Common Bonds

Common Bonds

Storytelling in the Classroom

edited by Alan Howe and John Johnson

THE NATIONAL ORACY PROJECT

Hodder & Stoughton

LONDON SYDNEY AUCKLAND

Cover photography by Colin Taylor Productions.

Illustrations on pp. 22–3 and 52–3 by Picturegraphics.
All other illustrations by Angela Martin.

British Library Cataloguing in Publication Data

National Oracy Project
Common Bonds: Storytelling in the Classroom
I. Title
371.3

ISBN 0-340-57308-2

First published 1992

Disc conversion by Columns Typesetters of Reading
Printed in Great Britain for the educational publishing division of Hodder & Stoughton Ltd., Mill Road, Dunton Green, Sevenoaks, Kent by St Edmundsbury Press, Bury St Edmunds, Suffolk.

CONTENTS

List of contributors   vi

Introduction   vii

About this book   ix

Chapter 1   Storytelling: weaving many threads   1

Chapter 2   Articulating experience   14

Chapter 3   Storytelling and the National Curriculum   28

Chapter 4   Traditional tales   44

Chapter 5   Storytelling and equal opportunities   57

Chapter 6   Resources for using and developing stories   69

LIST OF CONTRIBUTORS

Common Bonds: Storytelling in the classroom has been prepared by the National Oracy Project for all people interested in developing the role of storytelling in education. The writing team for the book was:

Angela Doogal, Co-ordinator, Enfield Oracy Project
Sally Elding, Co-ordinator, Cambridgeshire Oracy Project
David Horner, Co-ordinator, Cheshire Oracy Project
Alan Howe, Officer, National Oracy Project
John Johnson, Director, National Oracy Project
Kate Price, Co-ordinator, Walsall Oracy Project.

The National Curriculum Council and the National Oracy Project would also like to express their gratitude to the following for their contributions to this book:

— to co-ordinators, advisers and staff of the Council and the Project who contributed to the planning, writing and publishing of this book;

— to all the children, parents, teachers and ancillary staff whose ideas, activities and talk have been included here;

— to all the storytellers who have contributed to the development of our ideas.

INTRODUCTION

... narrative in school is not something to be consumed (in written form) but something to be made by every person in every possible way.[1]

Ben Haggarty, one of a group of professional storytellers known as 'The Company of Storytellers', talks about a 'Ladder of Stories' that characterises an evening's storytelling in communities as far apart as West Africa and Ireland. The evening starts, on the lowest rung of the ladder, with those gathered together, often around a fire, swapping anecdotes about the day just passed. These lead some to recall events from the recent past. Jokes are told, and the children, who are now getting sleepy, are entertained and educated through stories told specifically for them. As the night gathers, however, and the firelight grows dimmer, other stories emerge: family stories, brought out and polished for the hundredth time; myths and legends; stories of events and deeds performed long ago, much changed in the generations of telling; and finally stories that have their source in the great questions of human existence – those narratives which explain 'life, the universe, and everything'. These stories represent the highest rung of the ladder, but they share the same context and often the same features as those stories told at the beginning of the evening.

Over the last few years storytelling has been undergoing a revival, both in the classroom and in society as a whole. This has coincided with an increasing awareness of the value of the spoken word as a means of learning and as a way for pupils to demonstrate evidence of their achievements. Like the 'ladder of stories', this book exemplifies the variety of approaches to storytelling that teachers are using and also the connections that can be made between stories, pupils' own experiences and the curriculum.

When the National Oracy Project established itself in schools and education authorities, many teachers began to recognise the value of the narrative mode of language. They found ways of using narrative to enhance their pupils' learning. They also saw in storytelling a powerful context for the development of language (both spoken and written) itself.

The National Curriculum has clearly identified the importance of narrative as a way for pupils to organise their ideas and experiences in the spoken word. Storytelling, responding to stories, using the

---

[1] Rosen, H. (1988) 'A Postscript' to Rosen, B. (1988) *And None of It Was Nonsense* Mary Glasgow Publications

narrative mode to explore ideas and to consolidate and demonstrate learning – all of these are required aspects of the programmes of study in English.

At Key Stage 1 the range of activities should include, 'listening and responding to stories' and 'telling stories'. At Key Stage 2 to 4, pupils should be given the opportunity to, 'recount events and narrate stories'.

There are explicit references to storytelling in the statements of attainment for Speaking and Listening (AT1). Storytelling work can also contribute to pupils' achievements in other aspects of speaking and listening, and to their understanding of how language works.

Storytelling provides contexts for talking, listening, reading, writing and other activities such as dance, drama and design work. It is thus an ideal vehicle for covering a range of other programmes of study in a number of subjects. Storytelling is also a valuable activity in its own right and should not be regarded as suitable only for younger pupils. The experience of those teachers who have been working at Key Stages 3 and 4 suggests that narrative is a way of thinking that is ideally suited to handling complex concepts and issues. Barbara Hardy has called it 'a primary act of mind'[2]. It deserves a much fuller place in learning, alongside other ways of developing and communicating ideas more commonly associated with school.

---

[2] Hardy, B. 'Towards a Poetic of Fiction: An Approach Through Narrative' in (1968) *Novel: A Forum on Fiction*, Brown University

ABOUT THIS BOOK

Common Bonds develops a rationale for using storytelling in the classroom from Key Stages 1 to 4. It examines in detail a series of case study examples and also offers a variety of practical ways of using storytelling in the classroom. It is based on and draws together the work of hundreds of teachers from England and Wales who have been developing approaches to storytelling in all areas of the curriculum.

The book is divided into six chapters: Chapter 1 provides a conceptual framework for the rest of the book. It is based around a series of short quotations from teachers, storytellers, educationalists, and pupils, and identifies the ways in which storytelling is central to our learning and to our development as social beings. It defines storytelling as a broad and inclusive range of activities in which pupils of all ages can participate.

Chapters 2 to 5 look in depth at four areas of interest, using transcript material from children's and adults' stories. The material shows how important it is to reflect on what is being communicated via the stories.

Chapter 6 is a chapter of practical guidance which gives advice and further information to teachers and pupils, suggestions for working with visiting storytellers and for organising storytelling events. The chapter also contains a detailed bibliography which includes books for storytelling as well as books about storytelling, with some commentary on each.

A 60 minute video cassette is available separately as a companion to this volume; it features three detailed case study accounts of storytelling work at Key Stages 2 and 3. The video material is intended for use in INSET and for teachers wishing to see some of the approaches described in this book in action.

The examples of people talking in this book have been transcribed as they occurred, with no attempt to 'standardise' the language, even when there are instances of language use which most teachers would want to correct in a 'finished' draft, either written or spoken. The punctuation of these pieces has, however, been largely standardised in order to aid comprehension; more specialised conventions of transcript-writing such as indications of overlap, volume of utterance and length of pause have, for the same reason, been omitted from this volume.

ONE

Storytelling: weaving many threads

As the material which has been gathered together in this book illustrates, 'storytelling' is an umbrella term for a wide range of language activities. This chapter considers the views of many of those who have been involved in recent work in narrative. It develops an argument for giving a fuller place to storytelling in the curricular experience of all pupils. It examines ways in which the narrative mode can be built into the learning of pupils across the curriculum. Finally, the chapter proposes that traditional tales can provide pupils with a challenging context for the development of their oral skills, and a rich resource of stories for pupils to discuss, retell, rework and use as a stimulus to other work.

In this publication, the term 'storytelling' is used to refer to the full range of types of story, as discussed later in this chapter. The phrase 'traditional tale' is used to refer to stories from the oral tradition.

What range of activities can be regarded as 'storytelling'?

Roget's Thesaurus provides us with the following list of types of narrative:

argument, plot, sub-plot, scenario; historiography, history, annals, chronicle; record, account, story, tale, fable, tradition, legend, mythology, myth, saga, epic; allegory, parable; fairy tale, fiction, yarn; fable; reminiscence, remembrance; biography, real-life story, human interest; life, curriculum vitae; experiences, adventures, fortunes . . . personal account, autobiography, confessions, memoirs, memorabilia

The list suggests some common characteristics of narrative. But it also suggests differences:

- in the **form**. Compare, for example, a fairy tale with the ruminative account by an old person of an early childhood memory.

- in the **length** of narrative. It is interesting that 'anecdote' does not feature in the list from *Roget*, although many of the approaches contained in the rest of this book use it as the starting point for developing storytelling.

- in the **source** of the narrative. Some stories emerge newly-minted from personal experience, others as the retelling of a well-loved favourite.

- in the **content**. Again, think of the difference between a personal account and the full-blown recounting of a saga (where the forces of evil and good battle for supremacy).

Storytelling encompasses a wide range of activities, from brief anecdote to the fully-developed performance of a professional storyteller. There can seem to be the world of difference between a group of friends sharing a joke together, somebody describing a deeply felt emotional experience, a young child telling a bedtime story to a favourite toy, and a professional storyteller launching into a 45 minute version of a Russian wonder tale. More often than not, however, these differences lie in the *type* of story being told rather than in the manner in which they are told. Teachers need to be aware of the many different kinds of narrative that might be encouraged in the classroom and to consider how this diversity of 'story type' might be harnessed in the classroom as a means of learning.

The rest of this chapter examines some of the arguments for giving storytelling increased prominence in the classroom. It also considers a number of key issues that will face teachers who are planning storytelling work with their pupils.

Why introduce storytelling into the curriculum?

The major reason for finding ways of building work on oral narrative into the classroom is the power of the narrative mode to shape experience, and, in the process, to help pupils to find meaning and significance in it.

Stories and storytellers are everywhere – at the breakfast table, on the bus or train, in the playground and workplace, in the pub, at the party, over tea, before bedtime – and, just as potently, in our dreams. Barbara Hardy writes of:

> ... that inner and outer storytelling that plays a major role in our sleeping and waking lives. For we dream in narrative, remember, anticipate, hope, despair, doubt, plan, revise, criticise, construct, gossip, learn, hate and love by narrative.[1]

We find ourselves telling stories when we see our family again at the end of a day or when we want to find some common ground with strangers. Stories emerge at family reunions, at those focal points in the life of a family – weddings, baptisms, anniversaries, funerals – when it could be argued that everyone is involved, in one way or another, in bringing the story up to date. Stories are waiting in places and objects to be liberated by tellers: in the photo album, the video or 16mm film, in boxes in lofts, hidden corners of wallets; in objects redolent of memory – birth certificates, old letters, postcards, bits of jewellery, a collection of shells ...

Andrew Wilkinson provides us with a vivid definition of these kinds of narrative, in which most children have been involved all their lives:

> Home is a place where stories are told. This is a fundamental definition of home which is not in the dictionaries. A family lives by its stories. Without them it is without past and without future, without imagination, without vision, without aspirations.[2]

Narrative is probably the most common way of organising experience. Because of this, even very young children will know, implicitly, a lot about stories, how they are constructed, what to expect, how to respond. This is an ability that the school should be able to draw on and build upon.

---

[1] Hardy, Barbara. 'Towards a Poetic of Fiction: An Approach Through Narrative' in (1968) *Novel: A Forum on Fiction,* Brown University
[2] Wilkinson, A. with Davies and Berrill (1990) *Spoken English Illuminated,* Open University Press

Stories work by alternately stimulating and satisfying our innate human curiosity. We know what kinds of questions to ask because we know, all of us, a lot about life and also a lot about how the story presents human behaviour to us. And not just written, literary stories – conversation, gossip, anecdote teem with narrative energy; the skill with which we shape, present, perform our oral stories ('So *he* says . . . then *she* says . . .') is so commonplace as to never receive recognition for the accomplishment that it undoubtedly is.[3]

Stories will undoubtedly start to emerge if you prompt children with particular questions:

— What was the best present you ever got?

— Has anyone here got a scar? How did you get it?

— Was there ever a time when you were really scared?

— Can you remember the best/worse time of your life?

— Was there ever a time when you were really angry?

— Was there ever a time when you did something really stupid?

— Have you ever been involved in a dare?

Storytelling is a lifelong activity. The 'ladder of stories' – from the personal narratives fashioned from our own lives right through to the shared stories of our cultures – stretches from our births to beyond our deaths, as we live on in the stories people continue to tell about us.

> If narrative enables children to make meanings in language in a particularly rich, extended, complex and powerful way . . . then we need to develop much more inclusive theories of language learning . . . whatever lies at the heart of storytelling lies at the heart of language itself . . .[4]

Some argue that story is more just than one of a number of ways, along with argument, analysis, explanation, of organising experience. The developmental psychologist, Phillida Salmon, suggests that to live is to be in a narrative:

> Each of us lives in a story that is ours alone. It is this story which gives our lives their essential shape, defines their heights, their plateaux, their declines, marks out their movements, direction, changes in

---

[3] Horner, D. (1989) foreword to *One Good Story Gets Another* Cheshire Oracy Project
[4] Fox, C. (1988) 'Poppies Will Make them Grant' in Meek and Mills (eds.) (1988) *Language and Literacy in the Primary School* Falmer Press

direction. In living, we tell our own stories. Nor are these stories merely a catalogue of the events which occur within our life span. As the authors of our personal story, it is we who must select from the myriad happenings we witness daily, what belongs to the story and what lies outside. Only we can weave what we select into the narrative, only we ourselves can link what is happening now with what has passed, and what may yet happen in our lives. As authors, we have agency.[5]

If this is true, young people in school will already possess a 'deep structure' of story – a recognition of it, and an ability to use it in many different ways in their learning. Their experience of school will contribute episodes to their own personal stories. Giving plenty of opportunity to use narrative will help to enrich the curriculum experience of more pupils, and add a significant ingredient of positive achievement to the developing plot of their lives.

What can storytelling achieve in the classroom?

It can be a means of learning

Storytelling is a powerful way of helping pupils to learn in *all* areas of the curriculum. Because narrative is an universal way of organising events and ideas, it can help pupils to explore, shape and express their thoughts and feelings. Because they have to shape ideas through narrative, they can grasp and consolidate the ideas for themselves. This is why storytelling has a part to play across all subject areas of the curriculum. The case studies in this book (especially those in Chapters 2 and 3) provide clear evidence of the value of storytelling as a means of learning.

> Our natural response to an abstract idea is to find some anecdote – or story – to make it concrete. Stories are the bridge of abstraction.[6]

Oral stories, told either by the teacher, by a visiting storyteller, or by the pupils themselves, can also be a direct stimulus to other learning

---

[5] Salmon, P. (1985) 'Three Metaphors of Living' in Salmon, P. *Living in Time*, J M Dent and Sons
[6] Wells, G. (1987) *The Meaning Makers* Hodder and Stoughton

and activity. Story can lead into dance, drama, art, design, investigations, or into other language modes (pupils moving from, and comparing, spoken and written versions).

It can help language development

a) Storytelling and oracy:
   Storytelling provides a vehicle for a wide range of activities involving speaking and listening. Pupils can:

   - retell stories to different audiences;

   - help to organise storytelling events;

   - work collaboratively on reshaping and retelling stories.

In retelling stories to different age groups, they will be having to call on and develop resources of language. This may include the skills of taking on 'other voices' in retellings, and developing greater versatility as a speaker.

> Just as important as recognising and valuing diversity between speakers is the encouragement of versatility within speakers . . . for all speakers, even the monolingual, there is a range of varieties, or registers, that have to be mastered in order to communicate effectively in the various social situations that they are likely to encounter. Some of these varieties are acquired as part of growing up in the local community, but others need to be the subject of conscious attention at school.[7]

In addition, pupils will be learning to handle the predictability and formality of narrative. They will also experience the freedom that oral narrative offers for embellishment, alteration and invention.
   Oral stories are an accessible form for all, enabling pupils to work in a familiar language mode and providing direct access to the meanings held by the stories.
   Beyond the language learning involved in handling the vocabulary and structure of stories themselves, pupils will:

   - work collaboratively on stories;

   - plan and organise storytelling to other audiences;

---

[7] Wells, G. and Nicholls, J. (eds.) (1985) *Language and Learning, An Interactional Perspective* Falmer Press

– reflect on what they are learning about storytelling.

In addition, narrative – particularly the use of anecdote – can contribute to the development of other functions of language – oral argument, for example.

Deborah Berrill shows how, in the spoken arguments of sixteen year olds, anecdote was used to:

– validate a generalisation to 'bring it to life';

– precede the formulation of new generalisations;

– follow through the logical consequences of a generalisation;

– qualify generalisations in the light of experience;

– explore alternative points of view.

Berrill writes:

> Rather than being irrelevant tangents, these anecdotes and personal experiences have served the development of the argument quite directly, giving the students solid evidence on which to base their decisions and make their choices.[8]

b) Storytelling and literacy

In the classroom, oral storytelling should not be seen as an alternative to reading. If children are listening to, telling and retelling stories, this experience will be valuable to them when they encounter books, and start to construct their own narratives in writing. At a later stage of schooling, for pupils who are already literate, oral narrative can be a source of valuable work which involves, for example, turning a spoken text on tape into a written version.

c) Storytelling and bilingualism

Work in storytelling offers bilingual pupils an opportunity to bring both their language and their culture into the classroom in a positive way. Some pupils may be closer to a shared oral tradition than others. This can be drawn on in storytelling work. Parents and other members of the community can be brought closer to the school through the imaginative use of story, often becoming a valuable resource for stories themselves. The kinds of classroom activities associated with storytelling, such as taping anecdotes and working on them in groups, the telling and retelling of traditional tales, can be carried out in a variety of languages. Some stories,

---

[8] Berrill, D. (1988) 'Anecdote and the Development of Oral Argument' in Maclure, Phillips and Wilkinson (eds.) (1988) *Oracy Matters* Open University Press

especially traditional tales and those based on personal experiences, may be embedded in a particular language, and are thus best first told in that language. Pupils might also tell stories with a parallel translation into another language. The sharing of the stories themselves can be an excellent way of genuinely valuing minority language, culture, and experiences.

d) Storytelling and knowledge about language

The programmes of study and statements of attainment for Speaking and Listening from levels 5–10 require pupils to develop their understanding of the ways that language works. Work in storytelling, provided that it includes a strong element of reflection, will be an excellent vehicle for this. As a result of an emphasis on developing and telling oral stories, pupils will necessarily focus on aspects of spoken language such as:

- Language diversity (the possibility of including dialect or different languages in a telling).

- Change and consistency in language (What happens to your language when you 'update' a traditional tale? What differences can be detected between successive tellings to different audiences, and why? What features of a story remain constant? Why?).

- The differences between oral and written versions of the same story.

- The structures and conventions of oral narrative (such aspects as formal beginnings and endings – how many variations on the 'once upon a time' can the pupils find?).

- Developing the use of one's voice as a storyteller; experimenting with different pitch, or the effects of pausing; whispers, shouts, other accents, mimicry and so on.

Ways and activities in which storytelling can be used

Storytelling can be used to:

- allow pupils to learn and to demonstrate what they have learnt in a way that is revealing and motivating;

- give an opportunity for information, events, thoughts and feelings to be explored, shaped, organised and expressed;

- as a way of explaining their understanding of a process, such as the functioning of the human digestive system;

- as an outcome of work on a topic, creating a collaborative story which is designed to reveal their understanding of, for example, the causes of pollution, or of an historical incident;

- as a way of exploring the various myths associated with creation in different cultures;

- as part of building with construction toys;

- as part of role play in the hospital corner, cafe, travel agent, or in other thematic areas set up by the teacher.

Teachers might use storytelling themselves in order to:

- pose maths problems for pupils to identify and then work on;

- set up a situation in science in which pupils have to investigate a problem by devising and then conducting various scientific tests;

- provide an accessible explanation to pupils of a complex concept or process;

- set dilemmas for pupils to discuss together;

- help children to understand aspects of social behaviour through the use of stories which raise moral issues;

- share their own personal experiences with children in order to demonstrate common experiences or themes;

- enhance understanding and empathy through deeper involvement in the subject matter;

- give pupils a purpose for researching information, a context and a vehicle for using the information and making it their own;

- require pupils to order events and experiences, organise information and create a cohesive and coherent whole to convey to other people;

- give pupils the power to speculate and hypothesise about possible events and happenings;

- allow imagination and creativity to be combined with information and other skills to devise a product that is memorable and interesting to both teller and listener;

- allow a variety of issues to be explored and a variety of standpoints to be taken;

- provide a human interest element, which can include people's actions, values, attitudes, lifestyles and emotions;

- provide an opportunity for pupils to use a variety of skills, including home and community language skills.

Storytelling can be built into the following activities:

- visits or trips;

- pupils making tape-diaries when they are out and about, and then using these as the basis for developing more shaped narratives when back in school;

- as a way of debriefing from a period of work experience;

- as part of work in history – collecting the reminiscences of old people as a way into a topic, or in order to consider the question of what constitutes evidence.

What is the value of the traditional tale?

Stories were the invisible baggage of travellers, to be traded as entertainment for hospitality. For slaves stripped even of their language, the stories in their heads were all they retained of home ... Stories ... were rich, emotional, word-of-mouth tales handed down through the generations and told around the fireside. Many of them were ostensibly about life – unanaesthetised by convention – continuance and death, with the added ingredient of fantasy.[9]

A strong feature of storytelling work within the National Oracy Project has been the discovery for many teachers of the value of traditional tales as a stimulus to classroom activities and discussion. It might be worth exploring the reasons for this interest in traditional tales a little further. According to Helen East, a professional storyteller:

Storytelling is the earliest, and most enduring form of education; it has been practised by all peoples, in all parts of the world, ever since humans began to think and to seek to understand themselves and their surroundings.[10]

Many traditional tales deal with 'big' or difficult issues. The tales can

---

[9]Carter, Angela interviewed in *The Observer*, 21.10.90
[10]From Factsheet 4, The Education Programme, BBC

help us to handle things that it might be difficult to speak about directly or too literally. Very often these stories might show characters having to make choices, or suffering as a result of greed, or vanity, and so on. The narrative structure can give even young children access to these difficult ideas: for example, a five year old girl, after listening to – and participating in – a telling of the story of 'The Fisherman's Wife', exclaimed spontaneously, 'She wanted too much! She got power mad!'

The telling of a traditional tale enables the listener to be both a participant and an observer of the events. The imaginative visualisation that is required to listen well – no pictures, only words, gestures, rhythms – draws the listener into a story, but the presence of the storyteller also ensures detachment. The events and the feelings that they give rise to are contained in the telling, open for consideration.

Narrative is a good teacher: it is able to pose dilemmas, to reveal complexity in motive and choice, in feeling and action. It can also drop a line into our subconscious, give us a glimpse of other, more distant places and times.

> Once you enter the world of folk tales, you become part of a world philosophy. They are a complete way of looking at life.[11]

There are some difficulties associated with traditional tales. Discussion of them may sometimes need to focus on aspects that are problematical in themselves. A tale might contain gender or racial stereotypes (as in 'The Fisherman's Wife', a Grimms' story mentioned above), or actions that can be seen as morally questionable. The pupils' own retellings or versions might also exhibit these features. The fact that such issues might arise is no argument for proscribing such stories. The classroom needs to be a place where these kinds of dilemmas can be pondered and discussed openly. The teacher's response to stereotyping which is generated by pupils, for example, need be no different from a similar response to a written story. The author needs to be questioned about the portrayal of characters and actions; pupils and teacher need to be able to discuss such matters together. (See Case Study 1 on p.58 in Chapter Five for one teacher's account of how she has considered this issue.)

In addition, the kind of choices that storytellers make – which stories to tell, which details to emphasise, which aspects of the story to change, which to stay true to, need to be made available to pupils

---

[11] Graal, Kevin, professional storyteller, quoted in *The Times Educational Supplement*, 'Let's Hear It Then', 12.10.90

as well. We are not suggesting that you *should* make changes without careful thought, however. Changing the gender of the protagonist may fundamentally alter the meaning of the story: one of the reasons why wicked step parents crop up so often is because they're not blood relations, and replacing them in a story with 'brother', for example, can be deeply disturbing to people from some cultural backgrounds. The point is not that stories should be regarded as sacrosanct, but that the implications of making changes need to be thought through.

Developing a sense of audience

Storytelling is, ultimately, a social event. Stories were originally told by firelight, permitting eye-contact, with the sound of the human voice the central feature. Oral narratives demand a lot of both tellers and listeners. Tellers can develop a sense of their listeners which will affect the telling. The listeners will need to be alert to the nuances of speech and gesture that will bring the story to life. But there are advantages as well:

> In telling . . . one can shape the story to one's own needs, and while this may require the development of certain, perhaps buried skills, the advantages are very great. In the first place, one can address one's audience directly: one can make eye contact or not as and when one chooses, use gesture and mime freely, expand or modify the form of one's telling as the occasion demands, and in general establish and maintain a community of attention between teller and listener.[12]

Drawing the listener into the story helps the storyteller to develop a repertoire of strategies using voice ('sighs, groans, deep breaths, hesitancy, tongue against teeth, clicks of exasperation, contempt', as Helen East has written of her art).

For the teller, too, there is a special value in the act of telling a story many times, particularly a traditional tale. In an interview published in the programme to the Third International Storytelling Festival, held in London in 1989, Peter Brook, who has drawn heavily on traditional tale for his recent work in the theatre (most significantly with the Hindu epic, the *Mahabharata*) said this about the value of storytelling for the teller:

> I think that the whole question of quality in speech, quality in tone of

---

[12]Morgan, J. and Rinvolucri (1983) *Once Upon A Time: Using Stories in the Language Classroom* Cambridge University Press

voice, depends on whether or not a certain two-way listening is there. As you tell a story, can you listen to it so that there are two listeners? There's the listener in front of you who is hearing it maybe for the first time, and there's also the listener inside you, who's enjoying hearing the story for the hundredth time, lazily, like somebody who likes the sound of his own voice, but who has the listening of someone re-appreciating and re-opening himself to the story. Then there is two-way listening. You are listening to what you're telling to the other person and you are genuinely re-discovering it.

Teachers involved in the National Oracy Project have started to 'tell' stories to their classes. We hope this book will demonstrate that this is not a difficult step to make and that there is a storyteller in every one of us, whether teacher or pupil.

- There is a wide range of activities that can be classified as 'storytelling'.

- Narrative is a powerful and accessible way of organising and understanding experiences, and for this reason it deserves a place in the learning of pupils of all ages, across the curriculum.

- Stories may be generated from many sources. Three are likely to be particularly relevant in the classroom:

  - stories emerging from pupils' own experiences, or those of their families and communities;

  - stories developed out of the concepts, knowledge and experiences offered by the subject areas in the curriculum;

  - traditional tales (in books, told by visiting storytellers, told by the teacher, on tape or video; told by the pupils).

TWO

Articulating experience

Many traditions include tales which describe how stories first appeared in the world, and also how stories can be lost, destroyed or stolen, if they are not used and taken care of properly. The East Asian story, 'The Story Spirits', here recounted by a storyteller, is an example of this:

> There was once a little boy who was always told a story before he slept. However, he would never tell anyone else the stories he heard. The spirits from all these stories went into a leather bag hanging in the boy's room and, because he never shared a story, the spirits could never escape. As the boy grew up, the bag became very crowded and the spirits inside very angry. On the day of the boy's marriage the wickedest spirits agree to take revenge. An old man hears their plotting and all that day has to struggle to prevent the spirits ruining the wedding. When he has learned the truth the bridegroom promises that in future he will tell stories to anyone who asks him.

Stories have survived because of their essential importance to human life and because they are so central to the way we communicate with each other. And yet it is the pervasive nature of narrative that serves so often to lessen its value; in exchanging stories all day, every day, we render them, as Harold Rosen says, 'cheap as dirt'.

Nowhere is this more evident than with anecdote: personal narratives and stories which we tell each other to describe our own experiences. We grow apologetic if we introduce an element of personal experience into a conversation or discussion: 'If I may be anecdotal – just for a moment ...' In schools, which have traditionally placed a value on the polished, final – and usually written – product, this can lead to the virtual exclusion of personal experience from the canon of acceptable modes of discourse. As Rosen asserts in *Stories and Meanings* (1985), 'The further up the school system we go, the less likely is it that spontaneous, pupil-made narrative will be able to insert itself comfortably and naturally into the flow of talk.' Douglas Barnes makes a similar point in a contribution to *Language, the Learner and the School* (Boynton-Heinemann, 1990): 'because the teacher never asks questions that can be answered by anecdotes, anecdotes cease to be part of (pupils') own thinking about the subject, and become 'unthinkable' as contributions to class discussions.'

There is a falseness to this hierarchy of story. It is not, of course, a question of *either* argument *or* narrative, abstraction *or* concreteness, but rather of their interrelatedness and interdependence. In our talking together we habitually interweave one with the other. The generalities of argument and the particularities of narrative feed each other (see Deborah Berrill's comments in relation to sixteen year-olds in Chapter 1, p.7). Anecdote has a distinct linguistic existence of its own and a role to play within other language forms. The speaker who uses anecdote is not only developing a personal storytelling experience, but also an understanding of the place and purpose of anecdotal narrative in the modes of discourse, and the skill to operate within it.

Anecdote

Anecdote isn't simply a matter of the teller passively transmitting to another person material which already lies fully shaped in the brain. It is an active process in which we vigorously and carefully shape our stories according to our audiences and our purposes in relating the experience. Any groups of school children invited to recount why they were late in last night to a) their parents the following morning and b) their friends can vouch for the truth of this last statement! Articulating a personal experience gives the speaker a high degree of control over the material – it is, after all, his or her story.

The particular functions of anecdotal narrative for pupils would seem to lie in three interrelated areas:

- the stories we tell others to give shape and meaning to the experiences of our own lives;

- the stories others tell us of their lives which in turn become part of our vicarious experience and impinge on our overall ideas and attitudes;

- stories constructed out of or as part of specific school experiences.

The examples which follow show these functions at work in the oral narrations of a number of school children and their audiences.

Transcript 1
Helen's story

Helen is in a reception class. As part of the class's work in their first term in school, the teacher had read the book, 'When I was a Baby' with them. The children were then asked to bring to school four photographs of themselves as babies, toddlers, at pre-school age and now, at reception age. The children put these photographs into chronological order. Some children then took a tape recorder home to interview a parent or grandparent to find out more about their 'babyhoods'. The questions they used for the purpose were ones in the original class story, 'When I was a Baby'. Helen had first of all interviewed her mother at home and played the taped material with the class afterwards. At the end of the interview there is a pause and then the following:

> When I was born I could feels there was small. This is baby's. I wanted to know . . . how babies grew. I was in my mummy tum . . . I was in my mummy's tummy. I couldn't feel when the cream went in. When I had been taken out of my mummy's tummy I feeled ever so strange as though I couldn't breathe. I kept on crying in my tub which I slept in. My mummy kept on picking me up every time . . . I . . . It was morning. When I felt like the grown up, when I was two, I felt a bit grown up then to sit in the back of the car and to sit up. I couldn't sit up when I was one year old. My sister was born . . . borned . . . before me. First my Dad was born, and then my Mum, and then my sister and then me, because they were grown up when I was in hospital in my Mummy's tummy. My Mummy's tummy felt quite funny . . . when I was . . . only one year old.

No-one had asked her to do this. In the tape-recorded interview, Helen's mother relates the facts of Helen's babyhood and nothing more. Helen has then independently taken the opportunity to express what she thinks it really felt like to be a baby; this is her account of what her babyhood might have been. She uses the occasion of a conversation with her mother on the subject to continue to tell the story her way. She begins to explore and give shape to the question of what it means to be born and be a baby, and to her status within the family in relation to her parents and her elder sister. Thus we see her not just focusing egocentrically on herself ('. . . when I was two, I felt a bit grown up . . .') but also exploring and clarifying for herself through her narration the mystery of life before and during birth. She shows through her narrative what it means to have a position in a family and in a family history.

Transcript 2
Oral history

A class of Year 8 pupils was researching local villages near Marlborough as part of a combined Humanities and English topic. One of the activities involved pairs of pupils visiting local residents in order to interview them. Returning to class, the pupils listened to the interviews, chose interesting sections to transcribe, and then prepared a short talk to the rest of the class based on the interviews and the visit. Not all of the interviews resulted in narrative, but many did, and the pupils were asked to be on the lookout for stories, particularly from the older residents. The extract which follows comes from the end of a long interview with Bert, an eighty year old. Their teacher had given the pupils, Gill and Lucy, advance warning of one story that Bert might be willing to tell.

GILL: Well, our teacher said that when you went sledging, and there was a cow walking across. Can you tell us about that?

BERT: That's right.

GILL: What happened?

BERT: We went sledging, up, er, Green Lane, er, up past the stables, going up onto the gallops. We went sledging one moonlight night, and there were some cows in the field, and we came down, and, er, I got on the sledge and I came down, and there was a cow stood, er, you know, there's the cow stood, er, in that position, and I came down and, straight under her belly, straight through.

(*Laughter*)

GILL: Did she mind?

BERT: And the cow just jumped and ran.

(*Laughter*)

GILL: Who were you sledging with then?

BERT: Pardon?

GILL: Who were you with?

BERT: Oh, er, boys in the village, er, my age, but they've all, they don't live here now.

LUCY: What other things did you do?

BERT: No, some are dead, and others moved to different parts of the country.

LUCY: What other things can you remember you did when you were younger?

BERT: Oh, we used to go, we used to, er, of an evening, we used to, er, go for a good run, like, er, from down by the pub car park, right up round the common, down via Rockley, and over the downs and back

Storytelling and identity

Pupils learn about themselves, their backgrounds, culture and personal identity through research, experiences, emotions and events and through reliving all these in their imagination.

Pupils build a self-image and learn about themselves

The things I come out with are just about me.

I like to be myself.

I'm a fairytale sort of person.

We don't all want to speak the same language because we're all different people.

I didn't know I could do it, but now I know I can, and it's really great.

Teachers see pupils' identities developing and learn more about them:

– *'it was amazing to sit back and watch her talk for so long with such confidence ...'*

– *'I was surprised how articulate he suddenly became ...'*

Teachers have become aware that the pupils need the opportunities to learn about themselves through stories. These are things that teachers have said following sessions with a visiting storyteller:

'They've really got to start off with their own experience.'

'I've learnt that it's good for me to take part actively with what the children are doing. It gives them confidence to try new things and express themselves.'

A pupil reflects on her own development through storytelling:

Does it matter so much that I can't write very well?

Cos look at me now, I come out of my shell.

Teachers have learnt about individual pupils and aspects of their lives:

'The culture is part of their life and that is one thing that puts them together as well. I've learnt a lot. We each impart information to each other. You get the cultures and what's happened in their country . . . '

Watching a recent arrival in this country a teacher said: 'She did her story and she really came out, and that was lovely, it was good to see.' Also, concerning a Year 1 child: 'She was a school refuser. It was amazing to sit back and watch her talk for so long, with such confidence. She doesn't find a lot of the work easy.'

About the way that children used their experiences in storytelling:

The children were learning to cope with their private fears and worries. It helped them to learn about themselves and grapple with their emotions.

Following a 'dilemma' story:

The children were really questioning their values as individuals. They're having to think about themselves very deeply.

She told a personal story that was clearly very traumatic and she tells it over and over again to, mm, . . . she is slowly coming to terms with it.

I will definitely make more use of the things that happen at home or with the family.

Family life is a crucial key to the pupil's personality. Getting pupils to relate events in story form helps us all to know them better.

What do your pupils' stories tell you about their identities?

down, er, round that, down, er, that road on the other side of the church . . . and we used to get some old tin cans, frying pans and make them up into a band, and go marching all up, er, on Fridays, all up round the downs, playing what we called tunes. (*They all laugh*) . . . We played old songs and all that. Oh, we used to have a bit of fun.

By this stage of the interview, both pupils are on the alert for stories, as Lucy's question ('What other things can you remember you did when you were younger?') illustrates. What they get is a direct line into a piece of rural history. Bert's delivery is hesitant, no doubt the result of this unusual demand being made on him – he lived on his own, and was probably being asked to recall events of which he rarely spoke. There is no sense of a 'well-honed' and often-told narrative here. The pupils are hearing an authentic voice. Although this brief extract may not adequately reveal it, the two pupils show a degree of sensitivity and maturity in their questioning, to the extent that Bert is happy to talk freely about his childhood. Anecdotes, like all stories, thrive not only on good tellers and tales, but also on good audiences. Here the two girls provide that audience for Bert; he must relish re-telling the story as much as they enjoy hearing it for the first time.

We have selected this example to show that narrative is 'probably the most common way of organising experience'. Conversations of this kind reveal narratives that are always, paradoxically, unique and common. In meeting Bert, Gill and Lucy gain a glimpse into almost lost patterns of rural childhoods and lives. Their laughter together shows very plainly what all childhoods share in terms of adventure and comedy. It is a rich addition to both their learning and their linguistic repertoire.

Transcript 3
Nine fat frogs

The transcript below is of a collaborative story narrated by three seven year old boys following a trip to Chester Zoo the previous day. On the zoo visit the children had brought ice creams or iced lollies, some of which were in the shape of frogs. Rather than ask the children to write about or draw their experiences at the zoo, the teacher tape-recorded the class telling the stories of their day and making any comments they wished. During the lunch break the three boys made up a story about the zoo visit which they told to the rest of the class straight after the break. The whole narrative lasts well over six minutes, and we have included here just two extracts from the beginning and from the end.

Extract 1

JAMES: One day we went for a trip to Chester Zoo and –

CARL: . . . there was all these slimy – (?)

JAMES: No, no, yeah. And then we – and then we had some lollipops on a bench. There were nine of us, and the lollipops were on a bench. There were nine of us, and the lollipops were Fat Frogs, so we had nine Fat Frogs.

MATTHEW: Yes.

JAMES: And just near the beginning Micky said, 'I just thought mine blinked'. And then Matthew says, 'I thought mine just waved his hand at me'.

CARL: And I said, 'Mine, er – kicked me'.

JAMES: And then, er, everybody was shouting out that theirs was doing all funny things. And in the end they all hopped off. And one of them, got into the monkeys' cage and started getting the monkeys really angry. He's tightroped across the road – (?). And another got in the Koi carp and he got inside on the Koi carp and he froze the Koi carp.

MATTHEW: And my frog went up . . . rode round, round into this lady's knickers (*laughter*) and then this lady was going, 'Aaagh! Aaagh! Help me! Help me! What is that thing? Agh, it's a frog!'

Extract 2

MATTHEW: And then she faints and then she, and, the frog, one of the frogs went into this giraffe's erm –

CARL: – long head –

MATTHEW: – and then it was, he done a little ballet dance . . .

JAMES: – on his head, and then he fell . . .

MATTHEW: And he went into the Fi- Tropical House and he smashed a window and then the fish and then the frog eated all the fish. And then he was all fat.

(*Pause*)

CARL: And another one went into the Nocturnal House and he kept on teasing all the bats. He kept on pulling funny faces at them.

JAMES: When they were trying to sleep.

CARL: Yeah.

JAMES: And then another one got into, erm, hopped down the path again and got into the elephants and he climbed up his trunk and he slid down and he thought, 'That was good', and he did it again. But then as he got to the top he felt all dizzy and he fell down onto one of the baby elephants. The baby elephants felt all itchy cause he was on his back and so, and so, and he tried to suck him up into his tummy and he made a little house in his tummy. And then he got out in the end though, down his tail.

MATTHEW: – and then they all became fatter and fatter.

(*Pause*)

Storytelling and the local community

Some children worked on a long-term project to produce a children s guide to their town. This involved interviewing local figures such as the vicar and the postman and many other adults known to them.

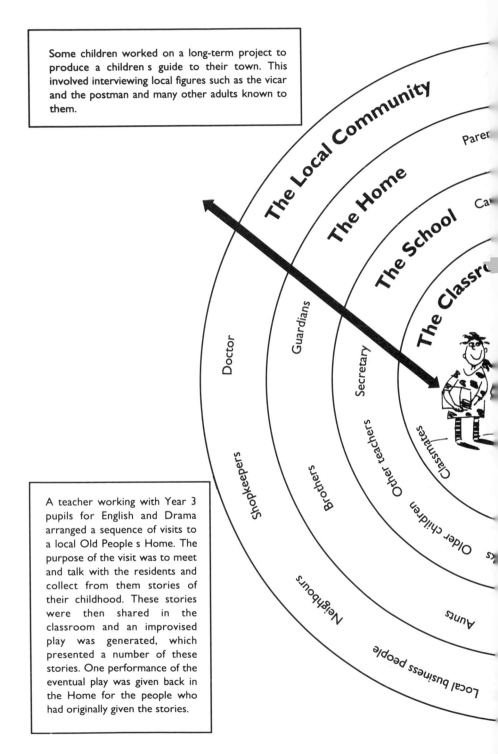

The Local Community

The Home

The School

The Classr

Parer

Ca

Doctor

Guardians

Secretary

Shopkeepers

Brothers

Other teachers

Classmates

Older children

Neighbours

Aunts

Local business people

A teacher working with Year 3 pupils for English and Drama arranged a sequence of visits to a local Old People s Home. The purpose of the visit was to meet and talk with the residents and collect from them stories of their childhood. These stories were then shared in the classroom and an improvised play was generated, which presented a number of these stories. One performance of the eventual play was given back in the Home for the people who had originally given the stories.

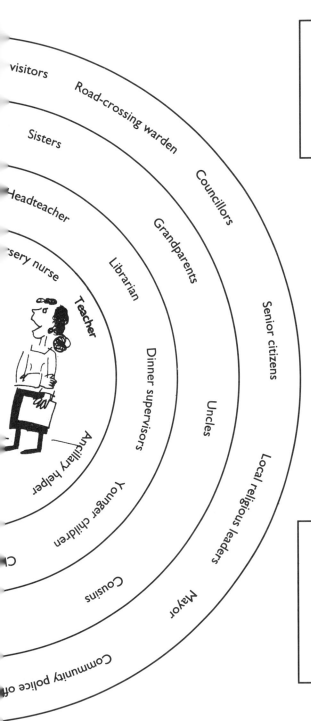

visitors

Road-crossing warden

Sisters

Councillors

Headteacher

Grandparents

sery nurse

Librarian

Teacher

Dinner supervisors

Senior citizens

Ancillary helper

Younger children

Uncles

Local religious leaders

Cousins

Mayor

Community police of

All the children of a junior school collected stories of the local community (from their parents, grandparents and neighbours) and contributed ideas and thoughts to a community play which they then performed.

A group of Year 7 children conducted a shopping survey and local history study including: making tape and video recordings with shopkeepers and shoppers; talking to Senior Citizens about their early memories of the local area; individual interviews with a member of the local community.

TEACHER: So what happened to them in the end?
JAMES: Well, they got so fat in the end that they popped and then they were just little frogs again –

In inviting oral accounts, the teacher allows Carl, James and Matthew to show just what linguistic and narrative powers they possess. The chance to share a telling also seems crucial to their success, as does the immediacy of an audience and its response to their creativity. Throughout the narrative, James is the most influential, controlling the storyline with some comparatively long turns. He had not, however, elected to work as a solo performer, though he may well have been the driving force at rehearsals! All three boys pick up and continue the story from each other in some remarkably fluent sequences of oral 'baton-passing'. Their story operates at three distinct levels: first, they transmit clearly the notion of a journey around the zoo. Second, they use that experience to intersperse some bizarre, even surreal comic episodes, no doubt Dandy-derived and rich in Freudian implications. Lastly, they include in their telling a number of items of specialist language, (e.g. Koi carp, Nocturnal, Tropical) which can only have derived directly from the previous day's visit and the knowledge thus acquired.

Transcript 4
Work experience

Work experience can provide pupils with a rich source of narrative. If pupils can review their time at work, selecting events, reflecting on and sharing experience, they will be starting to put their time into perspective. By listening to and commenting on each others' stories, the experience of work becomes less of a solo encounter. The learning that accrues can be broader than that associated with a particular job or set of workplace skills.

Following a two-week block of work experience, a group of Year 12 pupils spent a tutorial period telling and retelling elements of their experience to each other and in dialogue with their tutor. Angela has been at a local hospital. Her experience there included time in a geriatric ward and an encounter with an old lady who subsequently died.

TEACHER: Most of those at the hospital aren't ill, are they? I mean, they're in for fairly small operations, or they're there presumably for some time because they can't be looked after at home?
ANGELA: Yes, but most of the people in our wing were old, because the geriatric ward was full, so we had most of them in our ward.

TEACHER: There's a separate geriatric ward, is there?

ANGELA: Yes.

TEACHER: I didn't realise that.

ANGELA: Those people you have to do everything for, you have to feed them, everything.

TEACHER: And could you have coped with that, if you'd been there?

ANGELA: Yes. I went there for a week . . . I didn't like it that much, not as much as I'd liked it on the other ward.

TEACHER: It must be pretty depressing, because you know people are only going down, you know, but if somebody's in hospital, and they've had an operation, you know they're going to, you see them getting better, and then they go out, and you know they're going to be all right. . .

ANGELA: No, but this . . . the only week I went down there, they had a person die that night before, and apparently this was one of the ladies who could do something for herself, but she just slipped away in the night . . . (*pause*) And then there another lady, my mum was the home help for her, and, the first week I was up there she was in a wheelchair, and the next week she was in bed, she just went down and down and down . . . the next time they had her like in a hammock, just to stop her bed sores and things like that. She sort of kept on looking on and getting better and going back and getting better . . . and then she just went . . . in the night . . .

TEACHER: And could you cope with that?

ANGELA: Yes. (*pause*) It didn't sort of, I didn't pay much attention to her in case it sort of hit me, I just sort of went and held her hand or gave her a drink, didn't give her much attention, nobody did. The only time we sort of paid attention to her was when she had an injection, that was to sort of numb her brain so she couldn't feel any pain . . . she had cancer . . . cancer all over her body (*long pause*). It was funny at first, but I sort of took it in.

We suggested earlier that there were three territories for personal narratives within school. The first two promoted stories – our own and other people's – into the curriculum while the third took elements of the existing curriculum and turned them into narrative. This last would be done with the express purpose of allowing the teller to use the form to explore, shape, make sense of on-going learning experiences or to evaluate, reflect on and make further sense of previous experience. This seems to be exactly what Angela is fulfilling in describing her period of work experience to an interested and sympathetic teacher.

The role of the teacher in this is crucial. Notice how the teacher initially requests factual information ('There is a separate geriatric ward, is there?') but then offers Angela the chance to enter into her feelings ('And could you have coped with that?') and to follow this (almost certainly unconsciously) by the suggestion of a narrative structure for exploring those feelings further ('. . . if somebody's in hospital, and they've had an operation, you know they're going to, you see them getting better, and then they go out, and you know they're going to be all right . . .'). From this point, Angela moves into narrative. It's a reflective narrative; as it unfolds Angela selects and identifies the elements of the experience which are important for her: the irony that some 'just slip away in the night' when they 'could do something' for themselves; the need for those in close contact with the dying to keep a distance in order to 'cope'. The pauses, though, tell a different story. Angela is drawn back to the dying woman, and to her own feelings at the time. There is a quality of response here, a sense of a sixteen year old beginning to work at placing the experience for herself: it was 'funny at first . . .' but, through this narrative, we can sense Angela beginning to 'take it in'.

In considering these pupils and their very diverse narratives and purposes, our attention has been exclusively on pupils as storytellers. However, it is a truism all too often forgotten (or ignored?) that behind every successful pupil, class or school stands a host of skilled, enabling teachers; if our four examples do show successful children's work, then perhaps we should finish by attempting to pinpoint some of the ways in which these teachers facilitated worthwhile experience-based oral work.

- Creating opportunities and seeing a project through to a proper conclusion lies at the heart of this and all forms of oral work. Not only did Helen's teacher establish a framework for Helen's interviewing, she also provided the appropriate technical resources for Helen to maximise that opportunity.

- Human resources are also a vital ingredient: would the interview with Bert have been quite so successful had the teacher not allowed Gill and Lucy to form a working pair to support each other in what could otherwise have been difficult circumstances for an adolescent?

- Teachers offer an inevitable model for classroom behaviour. In terms of storytelling, it is appropriate that teachers on occasion willingly share with their classes stories deriving from their own experiences and on other occasions model the sorts of responses appropriate to the stories of others. It is the latter model that Angela's teacher so sensitively provides while Angela explores her period of work experience.

- We noted the quality of listening in Gill and Lucy during Bert's narration. An even more striking and salutary example is provided by the teacher of Carl, Matthew and James, who sits quietly and attentively by for five out of the six minutes' story! Only as she senses the story is drawing to a close does she help the boys out by asking, 'So what happened to them in the end?'

- After her interview Helen very much becomes her own audience, but in the other three examples, clearly, the teacher has either become (Transcript 4), formed part of (Transcript 3) or provided (Transcript 2) a real and sympathetic audience for the storytellers.

THREE

Storytelling and the National Curriculum

This chapter examines the place of storytelling across the whole curriculum. It may initially be helpful to think of storytelling as contributing to three aspects of learning:

- pupils' spoken language development and performance;
- pupils' development and achievements in literacy;
- pupils' acquisition, processing and communication of knowledge and understanding in a variety of curriculum areas.

In the first, storytelling clearly focuses on Speaking and Listening (English AT1). Substantial sections of the programmes of study can be met through listening to, telling and retelling stories. Learning to tell stories also encourages the development of a range of voices, registers, accents and dialects which can be used to effect in the telling, and the acquisition of a body of knowledge about stories – their content, their ways of representing human beings and their lives, their organisation and sequencing. These features will be apparent in pupils' retellings and can be used to build up a profile of their achievements in those strands within the statements of attainment which draw on aspects of language and presentation. Bilingual storytelling, in which stories are shared and retold in both English and other languages, is especially effective in developing pupils' confidence as speakers and their understanding of language.

In the second, the development of literacy, storytelling can be used to improve pupils' understanding of the symbolic nature of language, of how it represents human thought and action. This links well with the reading and writing of stories, and children's oral work can often be a valuable preparation for or an extension of their work on story in literate form.

Last, but just as important, storytelling can contribute to other areas of the curriculum. Because stories are used both to convey sequences of events and to represent symbolic meaning, they can help pupils to order, process and present their work in all kinds of fields:

— making up a story about historical events, drawing on their newly acquired knowledge of a particular event or period;

— preparing a story about a scientific or geographical concept so that younger children can understand the concept;

— telling a story which draws on number games relevant to the mathematics they are studying;

— turning their problem-solving work in technology into an amusing story for their peers.

The case studies which follow show how some teachers have used storytelling to develop their own and their pupils' work within the National Curriculum.

Transcript 1
Oral redrafting of story: 'Up and down'

Many teachers implementing the programmes of study for English have found it helpful to integrate work in all five attainment targets. In this example, one class of Year 2 children was developing stories related to picture books which they were making. One of the children, Peter (aged six), started to develop a story about two giants fighting over a flat on the top of a hill. He had already drawn the four pictures for his story (see p. 30).

Peter then proceeded to 'draft' his oral telling of the story onto a cassette tape recorder no fewer than eight times! In the process he revealed much about his understanding of story itself, and of how he could develop, add to or re-shape the story after re-hearing it on the tape. Here are two of the 'drafts':

Second draft

Once upon a time there was two giants. One was named Billy. He was very big. The other one was named Nick. He was in between big and small.

Billy had knocked the flag over. But then Nick realised, and he pushed it up and Billy fell down off the other side of the hill.

Then Billy pushed the flag back up, and Nick fell down the other side. The flag was sad.

Seventh draft

'Up and Down' by Peter. It was a lovely sunny morning and there was

two giants, one named Billy and one named Edward. They were good friends. They lived at either side of a hill. Billy had spent all his money to get nearer to the hill because of his friend Nick. Nick had built a house and he'd spent all his money on the savings of the materials to build the flag. He put the flag on top of the hill after he had made it. And then all of a sudden, because Billy was jealous, he started charging out of his house and bent the flag over.

Nick yelled, 'Oi, that's my flag. I don't want you to bend it.' Creak! then they were starting to squabble. They didn't like it at all.

Then Nick pushed the flag back up and he was happy. He giggled a bit because Billy fell down the other side. Edward was the flag. He was angry. So was Billy. Nick was very happy. They started to get angry.

Then Billy ran up the hill, pushed the flag over and Nick fell down. He was angry.

'Ow! I hate you.'

Then they started running after each other and kicking.

'Ouch! Don't kick.'

'Ooh, don't punch. That hurts. Ow!'

Between each telling Peter talked about the strengths and weaknesses of the version he'd just told. Thus in the second draft, the very opening ('Once upon a time') and the use of names ('Billy' and 'Nick') were additions which he had made to improve the 'story-line' qualities of his telling. By the fifth draft he had added dramatic dialogue, onomatopoeic words, personal attributes and emotions, and an explanation for the conflict. In the seventh draft, the previously 'monotone' relationship between the giants has become more complex, and the action is more varied, interesting and exciting. But the whole sequence of retellings does not indicate a consistent pattern of 'improvement': there were gains and losses throughout, and the eighth draft was not the culmination of all the previous drafts.

After the eighth draft (at which point Peter had always insisted he would stop his retellings), Peter's versions of the story were replayed to a group of four other children who discussed each version. They were quick to note the changes, and to comment on how they altered and improved the story. They referred back regularly to the four pictures, and they discussed the motives behind the giants' actions. These discussions prompted Peter to make further changes to his story when he completed the picture book.

As occurs often when talk is used to enhance pupils' learning and performance, Peter's teacher was surprised and delighted by the extent of Peter's knowledge and understanding, by the quality of his oral and written stories, and by the contributions made by the group of four children in their discussions. Within the National Curriculum for English there was clear evidence of the children:

- encountering 'a range of situations and activities' including 'working with other children and adults', 'listening and responding to stories', 'discussion of their work with other pupils and the teacher' and 'telling stories' (Speaking and Listening);

- hearing a book 'read aloud' and taking part in 'shared reading experiences with other pupils and the teacher, using texts composed and dictated by the pupils themselves' (Reading);

- writing 'individually and in groups, sharing their writing with others and discussing what they have written', and producing 'finished pieces of work for wider audiences' (Writing).

Transcript 2
Developing knowledge about stories: 'Three little pigs'

Stories are one part of every child's literacy experience. They hear and learn stories from their parents, relatives, siblings and peers, at first absorbing them aurally and then often hearing (and seeing) them read. Gradually they create in themselves the ability to tell sequential narratives, and to use language in meaningful ways within narratives. Teachers and researchers have often argued that this immersion in story is crucial to the development of literacy, particularly of reading, and to the child's success in school work. Gordon Wells, for example, states:

> . . . the child needs to learn to disembed his thinking from the context of immediate activity, and to operate from experience, both real and hypothetical, through the medium of words alone. Stories, and the talk that arises from them, provide an important introduction to this intellectually powerful function of language.[1]

In this example, a teacher recorded three children from one family re-telling a favourite story, that of the three little pigs. The tape recordings were shared with colleagues so that they could discuss the development of storytelling abilities in children of different ages. Each of the children had enjoyed hearing the story read aloud. The oldest had also read the story herself – including reading it to her siblings. The three complete retellings are too lengthy to include here, but we include an extract from each for comparison.

---

[1] Wells, G. and Nichols, J. (eds.) (1985) *Language and Learning: An Interactional Perspective* Falmer Press

Christopher (aged three):

Soon the wolf came to the house of bricks which the third little pig had built, em . . . he . . . he knocked on the door and said, 'Little pig, little pig, let me come in,' and the little pig said, 'No, not by the hair of my chinny chin chin I will not let you in.' 'Then I'll huff and I'll puff and I'll blow your house down,' said the wolf. He huffed and he puffed and he huffed and he puffed – wait a minute I need to do a wee – and he huffed and he puffed. The wolf was very angry but he pretended not to be. 'This is a clever little pig. If I want to catch him I must pretend to be his friend.' 'Little pig, are you ready, are you ready . . . ?'

Simon (aged five):

Next morning the third little pig set off at 5 o'clock. He filled his basket with turnips, then he hurried home. At 6 o'clock the wolf came to the house of bricks. 'Are you ready?' 'Oh,' said the pig, 'I've already been to Farmer Smith's field. I've filled my basket with turnips.' The wolf was very angry, but he still pretended not to be. 'If you will be ready at 5 o'clock in the morning, I will take you to Farmer Brown's apple tree to pick some red apples.' Next morning the third little pig set off at 4 o'clock. He was up in the tree picking apples when the wolf came along. The third little pig – the pig – was very frightened, but he pretended not to be. 'These are fine apples, Mr Wolf. I'll throw one to you.' And little pig threw down an apple, and it rolled away down the road. The wolf ran after it. The pig jumped down from the tree and ran all the way home, and the wolf was now very, very angry but he still pretended not to be. 'If you will be ready at 4 o'clock this afternoon, I will take you to the fair. We'll have fun on the swings and roundabouts . . .'

Katherine (aged 12 years):

. . . Then the next day early in the morning the wolf came. He knocked on the door of the first little pig's house. 'Little pig, little pig let me come in.' The first little pig said, 'Not by the hair on my chinny chin chin I will not let you in.' The wolf said, 'Then I'll huff,' and he puffed, and he huffed and he puffed but, and the house of straw blew away . . . the first little pig ran to his brother's house . . . and . . . stayed there. The wolf followed him and knocked on the door of the little pig . . . knocked on the door of the wooden house. 'Little pigs, little pigs let me come in,' he said. The two little pigs said, 'Not by the hair of my chinny chin chin I will not let you in.' The wolf said, 'So I'll huff and I'll puff and blow your house in.' He huffed and puffed and huffed and puffed. The house of sticks blew away.

The two little pigs ran to their other – their third brother's house. The wolf followed them again, he knocked on the door of the brick house, he said, 'Little pigs, little pigs, let me come in.' The little pigs

said, 'Not by the hair of our chinny chin chin, we will not let you in.'
The wolf was angry now . . . said, 'Then I'll huff and I'll puff and I'll
blow your house in.' He huffed and he puffed and he huffed and he
puffed, but the house of bricks would not move. The wolf was very,
very angry. He wanted his dinner how. So he had to think of another
idea. Meanwhile the little pigs were very hungry, the same as the wolf,
so the third little pig got a big pot of water and put it on the fire to
boil to make some stew. The wolf had a brainwave outside. 'The
chimney!' he said. He got up onto the roof, got his legs down the
chimney and let himself slide SPLASH right into the water. He
screamed for help but the wolf was no more. The pigs danced for joy
and had wolf stew for tea.

The three children remember and retell the story from versions
printed in picture books. Both the events in their narratives and the
words chosen by the children relate closely to the versions of the story
which they like. In Christopher's case, particularly vivid moments and
scenes are dominant in his story, slightly at the expense of the full
sequence of events. But his account still repeats the complex narrative
and dramatic voices of the story, with such sequences as 'The wolf was
very angry but he pretended not to be. "This is a clever little pig. If I
want to catch him I must pretend to be his friend"', moving from the
narrative event (he was 'angry') to the disguise of the emotion
('pretended not be be') – to the dramatised monologue of the wolf
('"If I want to catch him . . ."').

In Simon's case, the details of the story are more fully represented,
and the sequencing of events is more clear. The different times of the
morning rendezvous and visits to Farmer Smith's fields, or to the fair,
are now fully explicit, and their part in the story is clear. Overall, his
experience of the story in written form, and his commitment of so
much of it to memory through shared reading, have helped to develop
a complex retelling.

Katherine's story depends on a variant of the usual events – the first
two pigs flee to their brother's house of bricks, and the later part of
the narrative omits trips to Farmer Smith's or to the fair. Her retelling
is complete, yet compact – she renders the story fully but with hardly
a superfluous word or a hesitation. She has also adapted the words of
the original in order to make the retelling her own. She shows
complete command of the narrative sequence, of the repeated
encounters at each of the three houses, and of the language of the
original.

These three stories provide evidence on tape which could be used:

- to help you reach a fuller understanding of the development of storytelling ability in children of different ages, and of the role of reading in this;
- as part of a record of pupils' work for Teacher Assessment.

Transcript 3
Using narrative for conceptual understanding:
'The march of the electrons'

In the following example, a science teacher asked her Year 8 class to prepare stories for primary school children which would demonstrate their understanding of the flow of electricity through a circuit fed by a battery. She wanted to use the storytelling to assist her pupils in consolidating their newly acquired knowledge about electricity and in clarifying their understanding of the scientific concepts which underpinned that knowledge.

The pupils prepared stories which were made vivid by movement and by the use of props or labels to indicate electrons. They prepared them in groups and rehearsed them in their own classroom before telling the stories to the primary school children. During this rehearsal one group of girls told their story as follows:

> DIANE: Once upon a time in a long, long wire there were lots of baby electrons. Now these baby electrons were pushed down the long, long wire by the big bully battery's army of volts.
>
> SUSAN: It was a long, long journey down the long, long wire for the baby electrons and the baby electrons got very scared and held on to each other for dear life.
>
> RACHEL: The kind old bulb saw the army of volts charging the baby electrons down the long long wire so he kindly took them into his home for safety. The baby electrons were so happy they celebrated by dancing and using up all their energy. The kind old bulb was so happy to see the electrons enjoying themselves, he lit up with pleasure.

Questions were invited from the class. One pupil asked, 'What are volts?' The girls, after some hesitation, described them in the context of their story, as: 'soldiers . . . they push everyone around like a school bully'. Later, after all other groups had presented their 'draft' stories, they evaluated their own telling and discussed whether it would be understood by young pupils. They also discussed the fact that they had not included 'amps':

DIANE: I think we explained about volts. We didn't really need to explain about amps.

SUSAN: How would we put it in for little kids to say?

RACHEL: Exactly.

SUSAN: Yeah, cos . . .

RACHEL: I mean, 'amps' is sort or our age range, for learning about it.

SUSAN: You couldn't really put it into, like, a junior word, really, could you?

RACHEL: No, I mean, I don't really understand the amps measurement, anyway . . .

DIANE: Did you think we explained what the volt really was, cos it was an army, wasn't it?

SUSAN: We said it was an army of volts.

DIANE: And it was pushing.

SUSAN: . . . but we didn't actually explain what a volt was.

MARGARET: We could have made up . . .

SUSAN: Could have said, 'like an army of volts' . . .

MARGARET: . . . pushed them . . . we did, though, explain, didn't we?

RACHEL: We couldn't really have explained it any more. I mean, if you think about it, they might have thought, some people think it's like a school bully in a playground, and some people wouldn't have understood it at all.

After this review of their telling, the group of girls were asked to discuss what they knew about how electricity lights up a bulb. Their teacher joins them as they are talking about what happens when the battery runs down. At first she listens, then she intervenes:

SUSAN: We're figuring out how . . . where the electrons come from.

RACHEL: We're trying to work out where the electrons go when they run out of energy.

SUSAN: In Ian's play they said that electrons wear down and that they don't have any more energy.

TEACHER: And what happened to them?

SUSAN: They died . . . but then where do the other electrons come from to give more energy to the bulb?

TEACHER: Right.

RACHEL: They come from another battery.

TEACHER: What . . . forget about the batteries for a minute, just think about the electrons. Remember we did conductors and insulators?

RACHEL: Yeah.

TEACHER: What was the difference between them? Do you remember, Andy talked to you about them?

RACHEL: Oh, the conductors have got . . . solid atoms, I mean, free atoms . . .

TEACHER: Free . . . ?

RACHEL: Free electrons.

TEACHER: Right.

RACHEL: And wood and things, all the electrons are solid.
DIANE: They're all packed together . . .
RACHEL: Totally solid and you can't break into them.
TEACHER: Right, so for something to be able to have electricity through it, it must have, what?
RACHEL: Has to have free electrons.
TEACHER: And what do you mean by free electrons?
RACHEL: Electrons that escape from the atom.

Gradually from this point the teacher is able to help and support the girls as they bring together the knowledge which they already have securely and the semi-understanding which is emerging from their recent work. So the discussion with the teacher (too long for complete reprinting here) finishes:

RACHEL: So if you put another battery and it gives it more energy and the electrons just come back to life again?
TEACHER: That's exactly what happens.
RACHEL: They just like to go to sleep and then they wake up again.
TEACHER: Yeah, they either have the energy to move, or they don't have the energy to move.
MARGARET: And when you put the battery on again they start to go around in a circle again.

The emphasis in this example is much more on the role that the storytelling has played in developing the pupils' learning about electricity. Because they were asked to communicate their knowledge to another group of pupils, they had to identify the knowledge they held securely and the information or scientific concepts they were unsure about. This process encouraged them to articulate more of their uncertainty in their own review of their learning, and gave the teacher the opportunity then to help them towards fuller understanding.

Within the National Curriculum for Science in Key Stage 3 the children were clearly meeting the following aspects of the programme of study:

● Communication: Pupils should be encouraged to express their ideas by various means and to respond to those of others.

● Knowledge and understanding of science.

● Detailed provisions: Pupils should investigate a wide range of electrical components in electrical circuits, appreciate the need for a complete circuit, and investigate the chemical effects of electrical currents.

Transcript 4
Using story in the reflective process:
'Four-wheeled buggy'

One area where pupils are often asked to tell a story is in giving an account of their work: 'tell me what you did' or 'tell me what happened' may be the prompts to this kind of account. Yet pupils' responses to these instructions often disappoint teachers by being over-brief, lacking relevant information and, above all, failing actually to engage in reflection on the success or failure of the work and the reasons behind it. There are reasons for this. Pupils' responses are likely to be constrained if they think they are being evaluated and if they sense that the teacher knows more about the topic than they do. In this example, some of these constraints are reduced by the teacher asking the group of Year 5 children to give their account of how they made a four-wheeled buggy by tape-recording it for the rest of their class to listen to later that day. The work was part of a topic called 'On the Move'.

The three girls – Gemma, Liz and Ann – had been given the specifications, resources and instructions for making the four-wheeled buggy. Once they were satisfied that they could make the buggy roll they were to try to:

– make the buggy roll down a slope in a straight line;

– make the buggy safe on impact with a plastic brick wall;

– make the passenger (a pen top) stay safely in the seat (a small pot/box/etc) on impact with the wall.

Here are two extracts from the recorded account of their work:

First extract

LIZ: . . . and we got some small lollipop sticks . . . we got these small lollipop things and . . . we stuck the pieces of wood circles onto the lollipop things as the wheels with drawing pins.

GEMMA: Because first of all when we tried it the bull-dog clips kept leaning to the left and right, so we stuck plasticine on the middle and the outside so it wouldn't and that worked okay.

ANN: We tried three bumpers and the last one we tried, the one we've got now is a balloon and it worked.

LIZ: And we had . . . yes, we had to do this task and we had to make a seat and we had to put a felt tipped pen in it . . .

GEMMA: We used the lid of a felt tipped pen.

LIZ: . . . yes, and it had to be unsafe and . . .

GEMMA: Me and Liz had a massive argument about it.

LIZ: Yes, we had a massive argument, but then we decided to have Gemma's idea and it works.

Second extract

ANN: The seat it's on . . .

LIZ: It was a box, and we cut the top out and we left the sides and the bottom.

ANN: We put some . . .

GEMMA: We tried to put a piece of card with a hole in it, and then Mrs Elding told us the passengers had to be unsafe . . .

ANN: We was gonna cheat.

GEMMA: . . . the passenger had to be unsafe.

ANN: We cut a hole in it and we put that in there and it kept going under so I said, 'Why don't we put some plasticine?' . . . so we put some plasticine at the bottom, we put the pen lid in, but that was cheating.

GEMMA: Yes, and the box is still a little unsafe, because it's slanting to one side and we are trying to get it to the middle but it just won't go . . . and the piece of stiff card which is meant to be stiff card in the middle which the bull-dog clips are attached keeps bending and we don't know why.

LIZ: I tried it with a bottle top, the seat, and I put a rubber band round it to keep it on but they said . . . they, they had an argument with me and they wouldn't let me do it, so we had to leave it out.

GEMMA: We would.

ANN: We would, we said we had different opinions.

[*They stop the tape here.*]

Here the process of telling their peers the story of their design and development of the buggy encourages the pupils to explain things which had gone wrong and which resulted in changes in the design. They also admit (good-humouredly) that they did some things which broke the 'ground-rules' for their task. They raise their unresolved design problems: 'it's slanting to one side and we are trying to get it into the middle . . . and the piece of still card . . . keeps bending and we don't know why'. They recognise that each of the group has strong opinions which cannot always be resolved fully in the consensus needed to move forward confidently.

The work matches well the programme of study for the four attainment targets in Technology. The account is directly relevant for pupils working towards level 4 in Satisfying Needs and Addressing Opportunities:

Some cross-curricular opportunities for storytelling

English
Pupils should have opportunities to participate in all reading activities, e.g. . . . taking part in storytelling sessions. (AT2, PoS, Key Stage 2)

History
Schools . . . are likely to make use of . . . the following:
– presentation by the teacher, including storytelling. (Non-statutory Guidance, 8.1)

Modern Languages
Pupils should have regular opportunities to describe everyday activities and narrate events. (PoS, Model A, Key Stages 3–4)

PE
Pupils should be given the opportunity to describe what they and others have done in physical education . . . (PoS, Key Stage 2)

Mathematics
Activities should enable pupils to communicate their mathematics. Pupils need to . . . present and explain results to other pupils, teachers and other adults . . . (Non-statutory Guidance, 5.12)

Science
Children should have opportunities to continue to develop and use communication skills in presenting their ideas and in reporting their work to a range of audiences. (PoS, Key Stage 2, General Introduction)

Geography
Pupil should be taught to follow a route on an Ordnance Survey map and describe what could be seen. (PoS, AT1, Key Stage 3)

Music
Pupils should talk about music heard in class, including their own compositions and performances. (PoS, Key Stage 3)

Art
Pupils should talk about their work and how they have made it. (PoS, AT1, Key Stage 1)

- 'evaluate the outcome of their activity against the original need, and propose modifications that would improve the overall quality of their outcome'.

Some might argue that this account is not a story, that it does not foreshadow its ending in the constituents of a narrative as stories usually do. Others, though, would say that the sequencing of events, the engagement with the imagined audience and the commentary which accompanies the account, do merit the title of the story. The task has encouraged some relatively inexperienced speakers to draw on their experience, and to use narrative forms, to make a worthwhile tape-recording in what the programmes of study call 'a non-reciprocal situation'.

In considering ways of bringing opportunities for storytelling into schemes of work across the curriculum, teachers might address the following questions:

- Are explicit references made in programmes of study to possibilities for oral narrative?

- Are implicit references made to narrative in programmes of study – for example: 'give an account of', 'explain', 'describe'?

- Are opportunities for storytelling already built into schemes of work?

- Where might further or additional opportunities be created for spoken narrative as part of learning?

- What possibilities exist for using storytelling in order to provide pupils with special educational needs with greater access to the curriculum?

- How can stories be used to draw on pupils' knowledge, experiences and values, e.g. of their community or their culture?

- How might you recognise and use the understandings that pupils may reveal through narrative to contribute to teacher assessments in a range of curriculum areas?

- What possibilities are offered by storytelling (including the provision of other contexts for talk) for assessing pupils' work in Speaking and Listening (English AT1)?

- What possibilities exist for cross-curricular and/or cross-phase collaboration between teachers as a way of providing genuine audiences for stories?

- What resources – collections of stories, audio tapes (including those of locally-collected or pupils' own versions of stories) – can be built up to support storytelling work across the curriculum?

FOUR

Traditional tales

... if you tell stories and then begin to get the children to tell stories and write them ... by trapping this fundamental human characteristic, a way of thinking, a way of feeling, a way of delivering values, you release a quality of language that nothing else will release.[1]

A traditional tale belongs to the oral tradition of storytelling; it is one that has been handed down from generation to generation within particular cultures and from one culture to another. More recent additions to this tradition – 'local' or 'urban legends', for example – have developed and changed as society itself has changed.

Many of us have experienced traditional stories first in written form, printed versions of stories that were originally oral, often gathered by folklorists or anthologists, and often edited and re-written for a children's audience. There is currently, however, a dedicated group of storytellers, national and international, which has maintained and revived the art of oral storytelling, so that stories are, once again, no longer confined to the pages of a book. Storytellers from all walks of life are telling stories to audiences young and old, and the stories they are telling are drawn from all over the world.

Traditional tales in schools: planning and resourcing

This revival of interest in the oral tradition is of particular relevance to schools. There are benefits to schools in this wide diversity of traditional tales beyond the mere fact that the curricular requirements for English highlight the importance of 'folk tales, myths, legends' and 'examples from different cultures'. Telling stories to pupils, and

---

[1] Harold Rosen at a National Oracy Project Narrative Conference in July 1989.

inviting them to re-tell them to others, encourages them to become storytellers themselves. As the case studies in Chapters 3 and 5 also illustrate, hearing and telling traditional stories can help young children to internalise and use the structure and sequence of a story. Pupils will gain linguistically from the richness, structure and universality of good stories. Traditional tales also provide an opportunity to bring the 'home languages' of bilingual and multilingual pupils into schools in a way which validates their culture, enhances their own linguistic performance and increases the cultural experience of the monolingual students.

Communicating these stories to a new audience brings its own excitements and challenges. One parent, who was with a group of teachers developing storytelling, says of her own experience as a storyteller:

> I'm not a teacher – I'm not used by my training to sitting in front of a group of people telling a story, I'm not used to that kind of exposure and so from that point of view, it's almost, well, it's exciting.

This excitement, of course, is something that pupils themselves experience when they are encouraged to retell these stories.

Telling a diversity of traditional tales is a worthwhile activity in its own right. It is one, however, that needs to be prepared with care. Particular attention should be paid to selecting the appropriate time and place for the activity, making sure that there will be no interruptions, choosing the right story, creating the right mood.

The stories we most remember are the stories we hear. Nevertheless, a school that wants to develop storytelling should have a bank of resources which it constantly updates. The bibliography at the end of this book provides a starting point, and a rich variety of traditional tales can be found within such series as the Penguin *Folklore Library* (a seven volume series) and the Oxford University Press *Myths and Legends*. Picture books should not be neglected – there are some good stories in them – but written stories have often been adapted into a more literary form and are harder to tell than stories taken from storytellers. Collections of traditional stories on audio cassettes would add to a resource bank of stories, since they retain at least some of the elements of the oral tradition. (A selection of those currently available are also listed at the end of this book.)

Traditional tales in schools: activities and approaches

When developing work on traditional stories, it is important to ensure that the tellings and retellings are interesting, engaging and fresh. The following are some of the techniques and strategies that teachers in the National Oracy Project have used successfully to this end:

— Story Trees. A simple storyline with open-ended stages is used (say, four). The teacher pauses at each 'stage' and asks the pupils what happens next, noting down the pupils' ideas. This can be represented as a tree, with the 'branches' (the various predictions made by the pupils) springing out from the main trunk (the actual route taken by the story). A flow-chart is an equally effective way of doing this.

— Two different stories are told to two different classes. Pupils from the two classes come together in pairs (one from each class) and swap stories.

— The beginning, middle and end of a story are told to three different groups of pupils, who then join into groups of three to piece together the whole story.

— Pupils are told a story once and then have to retell it in a 'story circle', where the story is 'passed round' in one direction, the pupil on the left or right of the pupil telling the story taking it up where he or she left it off. The point at which each pupil 'hands over' the story can be selected by the pupil (the transference can be formalised by physically handing over a symbol: a conch, for example) or by the teacher (clapping or blowing a whistle, for example).

— Pupils are asked to 'freeze' a memory from the story they have just heard and to share it with a partner or partners, starting just before and finishing just after the frozen memory.

The examples which follow show some other approaches to storytelling in the classroom.

Transcript 1
Retelling and visualisation – a traditional tale

Danny and Alex are both six years old. The whole class had listened to their teacher telling them a version of an Anansi story, in which Anansi is asked by God to capture three things: a python, a leopard, and a tree spirit, in return for some stories. The story hinges on a series of tricks that Anansi plays in order to outwit the creatures. At the end of the story, the teacher wanted to help the children to begin retelling parts of the story. The approach she used was as follows:

— The children were asked to close their eyes and to picture in their minds one scene, or one incident from the story (they were guided in this by a few focus questions from the teacher).

— They then turned to the person next to them and quickly described the scene, and the action associated with it.

— They then moved to tables and drew their chosen scene.

— Once the drawings were finished, each child was paired with another who had selected a different part of the story. Each child was asked to turn the picture back into a story by imagining that his or her picture was a still from a film, or a video. The children had to rewind the tape a bit and then begin telling the story up to and including their scene.

Here is a transcript of Danny and Alex doing this:

DANNY: Anansi is talking to his wife and he ate some cow soup. So he went out and he had a great idea. Ding! His idea was, have a trap pit, really lots of honey around in the hot sun. Then he changed it into this nice drink, the leopard smelt it and so he came along to the entrance of his cave and he ate all the bowls. When he was going into the third bowl he went crash! He fell down into the trap, and Anansi was there and Anansi got two sticks and he went down the hole then. And then he got another stick behind his back and when he came up he went bang, bang, bang! So he fell back down and then he took it to his God and said, he said, 'That is very good, now you have to get, um . . .'

ALEX: . . . the tree spirit . . .

DANNY: 'The tree spirit.' So he went to get the tree spirit. He went back to God again. 'You have done very well, and what do you want in return?' He said, 'Some books.' And so he went down the spider's web with the books and then he fell back down it and went back to his wife . . . and that's the end of the story.

ALEX: One day there was this boy Anansi, um, and he wanted some stories for all the animals. They were fighting. And so he went up to ask God . . . umm, 'Can I have some stories?' But God said, 'You don't get them free.' So God said, 'You've got to get the python, the leopard, and the tree spirit.' So he went to get the python. He ate some cow feet soup. Ding! 'I've got an idea.' His idea was — he was pretending to say, he was pretending to be talking to his wife. And he was saying to his wife, 'I bet this string is longer than the python.' And his wife is saying 'No, it isn't, I bet the python is longer.' And then the python came slithering out. And then Anansi got some, got the string behind her back, and she tied it on the front, the middle and the back. And then Anansi strangled the python, and then Anansi took it up to God and he said, 'You have done very well', and that's the end of the story.

One of the 'tricks' about retelling stories is to try to remember pictures, not words. Here, both Danny and Alex are able to retell their section of the story in detail, primarily because the preceding activity had focused their minds on pictures. We can also see that both children are able to use their visualisation, and the drawing that they've made, as useful 'props' for their retellings.

It might be worth considering whether the differences between these two retellings are differences of style, content, or ability. Alex's narrative appears to be more tightly structured than Danny's: he includes more background information at the start, elaborating on the action preceding the scene where the python is finally captured. He appears to be a more assured storyteller than Danny, whose delivery is more hesitant. Alex is aware of the need for a degree of explicitness: 'So God said . . .', 'And his wife is saying . . .', 'And then Anansi . . .'. Danny's narrative becomes a little confused towards the end, with a number of apparently ambiguous references to 'he . . .'. But we need to remember the context: the boys were retelling the story to a partner who had heard it before. The pictures that prompt the retellings are in front of the children. It is quite likely that Danny is, if not pointing to the various characters, at least expecting Alex to know who he is referring to.

Both boys exhibit a strong grasp of a simple narrative structure, most obviously revealed towards the end of each retelling in the repeated 'And then . . .'. Interestingly, there is evidence that Danny is struggling towards a more sophisticated narrative structure in his use of 'When . . .' in 'When it changed into this nice drink, the leopard smelt it and so he came along to the entrance of the cave and he ate all of the bowls. When he was going to the third bowl . . .'.

In this instance, both children have a recently told story to work on. The visualisation work that they have done enables them to remember pictures rather than words and so retell the story 'in their own words'. They are not required to retell the whole story, but only one piece of it. They are in pairs for this retelling and so are not constrained by having to retell the story in public (notice how Alex supports Danny when he hesitates). Freed from the need to 'invent' the story, they are able to focus instead on detail and on characterisation. Both use direct speech; both show a fine grasp of what is a complicated narrative. Both might well be ready now to take part in a more public retelling of the story around the class, or to move on to writing a version of the story.

Transcript 2
'The Lute Player'

A group of eight Year 6 pupils had been told an incomplete version of the folk tale, 'The Lute Player'. In pairs, the pupils were asked to discuss the tale and to work out an ending. Each pair then joined another pair and shared their endings; they then chose one to retell. Each group of four put the whole story together and then retold it to three different audiences. The first audience was the other group of four who were working on the same material. The second was as part of a rehearsal for the final telling. The third audience comprised four other pupils from a different class.

Here is Amy, the first of her group, telling the other group of four:

> A long time ago there was a king and queen who lived quite happily in a kingdom, quite far away from here. They lived, they had everything they wanted. One day the king, one king used to have lots of, um, people coming for jousting and different activities. One day the king was very bored and decided that he would go on a journey to a bad king that lived across the des ... a des ... like a ... like a desert. He travelled with his army quite a far way, but somebody had told the bad king that they were coming, so the bad king got all his soldiers, rounded the mountain that the others said where he lived and so they were all ready for when the good king came, that they would attack. The good king travelled day after day, soon they arrived to the mountain, and all the bad king's soldiers came out ... and they attacked, and all the good king's soldier's got killed, and the good king was captured.

This retelling is within an hour of Amy hearing the original story. She is still struggling to get the events into the right chronological sequence, and to organise the details. The momentary hesitations are a sign that she is still 'remembering', and that this is a first attempt at putting the story together. Some of the slightly clumsy phrasing might also be the result of this.

After some discussion of their first attempt, the group had another go, this time as a rehearsal for their telling to the live audience. Amy is still the opening storyteller:

> There was once a king and a queen that lived in a small palace in a kingdom. The king used to arrange all different events in his palace. One day he decided that he wanted to go and joust with the bad king.

He travelled for many days along the dirty, dusty road. Soon he came to a mountain. On the opposite side was the king's pal . . . the bad king's palace. But, trouble lay ahead. The bad king had set all of his soldiers around the mountain so that they could not pass. There was a big battle. Most of the good king's men got killed – there was only him. He got captured and put in prison.

The changes are remarkable, especially given the limited time and discussion that the pupils actually spent on revising the story. Amy's narrative covers the opening of the story much more efficiently. The scene is set, the king is on the road and has arrived at the bad king's kingdom within the space of three sentences. Amy is much more in control of the events of the story, and is thus able to engage in that 'listening to oneself' that we are arguing is such a feature of good storytelling. She is starting to employ some of the rhetorical devices of the storyteller: 'But, trouble lay ahead'. This assured and economical telling emerges as a result of the insistence that the pupils work on successive retellings of the story and that they reflect explicitly on their first telling; it is also because Amy feels secure and confident in her group. It is a compressed telling, setting the scene so that the others in the group can be quickly brought in and the story 'proper' can begin to unfold.

Later that day, the third retelling took place, this time to a small group who hadn't heard any of the story before. Once again, Amy starts off:

There was once a king who lived in a kingdom, a small kingdom. He was really quite happy, and the king used to invite loads of people for jousting. One day, when the king was really bored, he decided that he would go out on his travels. So, he got together a big army and planned that he would go to see a bad king that lived across the desert. So he got his army and went off along the desert. When he had been across many rivers and streams . . . he came to a big mountain, just on the other side of the mountain was where the bad king lived. The bad king had heard and had got his army around, around the mountain, so when the good king came, he, the bad king, was planning to capture him. So there was this big battle between the bad king's men and the good king's men. All the good king's men got killed, except the king, and he was taken to be a slave.

In this version, the economy and control of the second version have been replaced by a fuller exposition. The rhetorical device that we saw in the second version no longer features, and, generally, Amy's third version seems to be closer to her first retelling.

The demands of the live audience may be the reason for these changes. Amy is making instant decisions to tell the story in a particular way as a result of her sensitivity to those listening. For example, the loss of 'tightness' in the structure, the decision to draw out the opening, might be the result of a desire to allow the listeners time to get into the story. Amy's increased sense of audience may also account for the greater emphasis on motive in this final version. We are told that 'the bad king had heard . . .' and was 'planning to capture . . . the good king' – details that were omitted in the second version. The transcript fails to reveal a further piece of evidence in support of this theory. The third retelling is considerably slower, with more frequent pauses. She is clearly 'pacing' the telling, possibly looking directly at her listeners and interpreting signs from them that she should slow the story down. On paper, then, the third version may appear to be a step backwards. But this is perhaps an illusion created by the written word. Amy's second version conforms more to the conventions of a written text. When she is telling the story for real, the different features of the spoken language – the use of repetition, of a more sequential narrative structure, the deliberate use of hesitation and pausing – come to the fore.

Transcript 3
Using local legends

Helen East, working as a visiting storyteller at a school in Yorkshire, describes how she managed to convince an initially recalcitrant class of Year 10 pupils that they also had stories to tell:

> The group was initially very sceptical about the whole idea of 'telling stories', but was fairly soon happy to narrate short anecdotes, personal or secondhand, that were essentially true occurrences. My problem lay in getting them to enter 'the world of make-believe' of folktales and comparable narrative, and to develop dialogue, plot, character and imagination in their tellings. Urban myths seemed to provide the bridge we needed between fact and fiction, the ordinary and the extraordinary.
>
> I told them a personalised version of the 'Vanishing Hitchhiker', and then showed the group the text printed below.'

The Everingham ghosts
PC Moody was riding his bicycle from the village of Everingham in the direction of Pocklington late one evening a year or two before the outbreak of the Second World War. He had not gone far from Everingham – not quite as far as the left turn into Hayton Lane – when he saw a figure dressed in black approaching him from the opposite direction and, apparently, also mounted on a bicycle. He noticed that the cycle had no lights, but its rider had taken him so by surprise appearing suddenly from the darkness that the figure had passed him before he registered the fact. PC Moody set off in official pursuit behind the

Working with a visiting storyteller

1

Points to be considered and discussed with a visiting storyteller prior to working:

- If the visiting storyteller is professional, you will need to budget for fees, travel and incidental expenses such as tapes, photos, etc.
- What role will you adopt in the storytelling sessions?
- What amount of time and space will be used?
- Which areas of the curriculum may be enhanced?
- What areas of need for pupils' learning and development are there?
- Are there issues of race and gender which may arise?
- What use may be made of pupils' own experiences of culture and language?
- How will the pupils be grouped?
- What is the contribution the storyteller will make to INSET?
- How will the work be followed up and evaluated?

Be prepared to participate and form a partnership with the storyteller.

2

The materials brought by the storyteller may include a fund of stories relevant to a wide range of events, and may include the following:

- traditional tales, myths and legends;
- dilemma and problem stories;
- collaborative storymaking;
- stories in various languages;
- stories using music and/or drama;
- stories about local history, people, events;
- stories reflecting various aspects of the curriculum.

3

These are some of the outcomes that may be expected from the pupils:

- use of own stories reflecting identity and culture;
- use of languages and dialects other than Standard English;
- development of storytelling techniques;
- telling stories to other children in the school, and to other audiences;
- oral redrafting of stories to polish them and improve them;
- ways of moving from oral to written versions of stories;
- organising events mentally through story to make sense of them
- collecting stories from family and community;
- exploring story development through music, drama or art;
- finding ways, with the teacher, into all areas of the curriculum;
- reflecting on what they have achieved.

4

Throughout the session teachers will be able to find out more about their pupils. They will have opportunities to observe individuals and to:

- keep a record of pupils' storytelling work:
- build on the stories which are told in developing aspects of the curriculum;
- foster a positive atmosphere for talk in the classroom;
- praise and encourage oral work and achievement;
- reflect on what has been achieved.

offending traveller. Although he had not seen the rider's face he knew intuitively that the figure was female. As he endeavoured to overtake the miscreant the cyclist abruptly turned left off the road, apparently heading toward a wood. Then the figure vanished. PC Moody felt a sudden tremor of extreme cold, and the hair on the back of his neck stood on end.

Disturbed by the incident the constable searched for evidence of the identity of the phantom cyclist. Eventually he learned that a girl had been killed on this same stretch of road some years earlier. There had been later, confirmatory sightings: the figure is always on a cycle which has no lights and is always in black. Hence the reason for her being knocked down and killed by a passing motorist. But it is the place at which the phantom cyclist turns from the road which is as significant as the ghost itself. There is only one possible place to turn: into an old gateway at the end of the high brick wall of Everingham Park — and this gateway leads into a wood.

In small groups, (each with a tape recorder) they then told similar stories that they had heard. I also gave out texts of some twenty other urban myths for those who really couldn't think of a story of their own. Initially these were used, but were gradually forgotten as story begot story, and a large number of very different stories were generated. These stories were then retold in other groups, the storyteller being free to tell their own story, or one that they'd just heard.

Here are transcripts of two of the first tellings in small groups:

Well, you know how Hugh works at Derwent Plastics? Well . . . Hugh went down one night just to catch up on some extra work, and he walked in the main room, and saw, like, this part . . . well, from about here upwards . . . of a Roman soldier, just walking straight along . . . and like you'd only see half of it because the Roman road was lower . . . he just sort of saw the top half of him.

There was this farm near us and thirty years ago there was this farmer and he was just taking his tractor back to t'farm and, er . . . he pulled into the barn and the barn, er . . . the barn blew up and he died. And today on the same day every year you can see the tractor going into the barn and in the same position, and, er . . . the fella's all blown up.

The next transcript is of a pupil retelling a story she'd previously told to a different group (the details are not the same as that told by the visiting storyteller — this is yet another version of 'The Vanishing Hitchhiker'!)

Well . . . you know the viaduct in Stamford Bridge? Well, you know it's been out of use for, well, years and years and years? Right. Well, there was this man and he was in his car and he decided to take this short cut home. So he did. Well, it was early dawn and he was half asleep and sort of a bit drowsy and he suddenly woke up when he saw a young girl standing on the highway there and she wasn't wearing much, just a sort of gown. So he stopped and asked if he could help her. She said that her date had got mad when she'd stopped his advances and made her get out and walk. So he offered her a ride home, right, and she accepted. She didn't say much on the way. Anyway, when they got there, to her place, he opened the door of the car to let her out, and she wasn't there. There was nobody there. So he went up to the door and asked if Mary was there, that was her name, right? And this old woman answered the door, and she says, 'Not again!', because this lass had been killed in a car a while back, and he was about the fifth person in eight years that had tried to bring her home.

This trading of stories which Helen describes often signals the moment when the potential of and for storytelling within a class is being realised: when the pupils recognise that they have stories to tell and also the ability to tell them. It is at such a moment that the teacher and/or storyteller can push the work forward into more traditional forms of story, or into other related work, perhaps involving reading, writing, drama or media work, on similar themes or topics.

In this chapter we have suggested ways in which the starting point of a traditional tale can provide powerful and accessible contexts for spoken language development and for pupils' growing awareness of the art of storytelling.

The following points summarise what work with traditional tales can offer pupils:

- the possibility of broadening the pupils' cultural experience and thereby of increasing their understanding of the world;

- the opportunity for the positive reinforcement of the spoken language abilities of bilingual and multilingual pupils;

- a linguistic challenge, which arises as memorable stories are told, listened to, and then retold to different audiences;

- the opportunity to develop awareness of different types of narrative (fable, folk tale, legend, myth, saga, tall tale, epic) as part of Knowledge about Language work;

- a genuine sense of achievement, based on the above factors, in which pupils can learn to hold an audience, develop and exploit non-verbal expressions and gestures, sustain a telling, and gain positive feedback from their listeners.

In order to help pupils to achieve the above, teachers will need to consider ways of building up resources of traditional tales, developing their own expertise as tellers and that of visiting storytellers. Chapter 6 provides suggestions for work of this kind and a bibliography which includes books *on* storytelling, books *of* storytelling and audio resources.

FIVE

Storytelling and equal opportunities

The development and use of spoken language carries with it issues of equal opportunities. Talking and listening are significantly affected by such factors as:

- the balance of power between those communicating;

- the constraints of peer group pressure;

- the varieties of language used and understood by pupils;

- physical disabilities or emotional factors which might affect pupils' willingness or ability to participate in conversation;

- gender;

- ethnicity.

It is very often in talk that such factors become apparent. However, one of the most significant contributions that oracy has to make to the provision of opportunities for the learning of all pupils is a range of strategies which can redistribute the conversational initiative, encourage diversity in language use, and provide greater access to learning. Storytelling offers a particularly powerful context for realising the potential of all pupils.

If, as we have argued, storytelling and storymaking are essential aspects of the psychological and linguistic development of all children, then all children must be offered the opportunity to develop and exploit these skills to the full. Previous chapters have already offered the case for using stories in many curriculum areas, and for a variety of purposes. In this chapter, we will focus a little more on the particular needs of certain groups of children, or individuals, and show how some teachers and storytellers have addressed storytelling and equal opportunities.

Case Study 1:
Storytelling and Stereotyping

Many writers have commented on the ways in which we use stories to make sense of our world, to develop and share our understanding, and to build a sense of identity. Gordon Wells (1987) writes that, through sharing stories, 'members of a culture create a shared interpretation of experience, each confirming, modifying and elaborating on the story of the other ... it is very largely through such impromptu exchanging of stories that each one of us is inducted into our culture ...'. This cultural induction may also, however, involve a stereotyping of human behaviour, most notably in the area of male and female roles, but also in terms of race, social class and grouping, geography (town vs country, for example), and so on.

The stereotyping of behaviour according to gender has been especially investigated in the area of storytelling, because women are often presented as subservient to men in traditional tales. This presents two problems, both significant. Girls' and women's roles and behaviour in society are now much more varied and complex than in the societies which originally told the stories and in those which gathered and committed the stories to written text. By the same token, stories which present ideals of male behaviour as aggressive, strong in fighting and seeking always to establish and maintain power within relationships, do not help support boys who are more collaborative and respectful of others. One teacher and storyteller, Cristina Bennett, explains how she has addressed this matter:

> A class of Year 10 Humanities students was looking at a topic on sexism; one of the options they chose was to investigate gender stereotyping in traditional tales. Having researched various aspects of versions of Cinderella, their brief was to write, or tell, a 'non-sexist' story, set in the past or present.
>
> As a starting point, I told a version of the Cinderella story (based on Charles Perrault's version). We discussed the similarities and differences between this one and the versions the class knew; then, in pairs, the group traced the pattern of the storyline. Each pair then chose a particular part of the story within which to explore two of the characters in more detail. We used a variety of strategies for this, one of which was hot-seating (a drama method in which students are questioned in role by other students).
>
> This is a helpful and valuable way in and out of characters – developing them as personalities with values and attitudes – and it encourages the character to consider what it is that they really represent. From this, students can decide whether or not to change aspects of the character's behaviour, or attitudes.

Once the pairs had sufficient ideas about the characters in the story, they then read a few other versions of the same, or very similar, stories to get a clearer idea about story language, story settings, and any changes to do with times and place. I had available: two versions of Charles Perrault's Cinderella, one from *The Fairy Tale Treasury*, selected by Virginia Haviland (Picture Puffin), and the other from *Cinderella or the Little Glass Slipper* by Charles Perrault (Picture Puffin); and two versions of Tattercoats, one from *English Fables and Fairy Stories*, retold by James Reeves (Oxford University Press), and the other from *Folk Tales of the British Isles*, edited by Michael Foss (Macmillan).

I used the Jigsaw strategy for groups reading these different stories. With this strategy, roles, questions or tasks are given to the class by the teacher. Students are grouped first in 'home groups' for the main part of a task, where they decide who will tackle which role, question or task. Then 'expert groups' are formed out of all the students with one specific role, etc; in these expert groups, students gain particular expertise which they then bring back to the task. Each expert group had to gather details of:

– where and when the story took place;

– any notable descriptions of time, place or characters;

– brief descriptions of major and minor characters.

Once back in home groups, students shared the common features and differences they'd found. These home groups brainstormed several ideas for changes to the story and began first drafts.

Students in some groups chose to work independently, others in pairs. (It is important to allow for such flexibility when much of the work has so far been collaborative; some students do prefer to work alone after a period of collaboration.)

The first drafts varied: some were storyboards; some were extended brainstorms; and others involved picture drafting.

At the beginning of the following session, I read the class Maeve Binchy's 'Cinderella Re-examined' (from *Rapunzel's Revenge – Fairytales for Feminists*, Attic Press). They discussed this as a whole group before returning to their first drafts to make any adaptions, adoptions or additions.

Drafting continued throughout the fortnight that this option ran. Some students chose to use their pieces for inclusions in their GCSE coursework.

The stories were shared around the class in a variety of ways:

– some were read onto tape and displayed along with other collections of stories for listening to;

– some were read by various groups informally;

– some were read to the whole group by the author(s);

– some were told live to the whole class.

Cristina has worked on this topic with children of many ages. With Year 2 children, for example, her aim was 'to develop the notion that females in stories can overcome difficulties without having to call on males to rescue them'. In her work with Year 6 children, she is 'more inclined to draw their attention to stereotyping by encouraging them to question the portrayal of the characters and look at what's behind storylines and patterns'.

Cristina concludes:

> These few examples show some ways in which the whole topic of gender stereotyping can be approached through oral storytelling. It is easy to be ambitious for our children to become critical, but this should not be at the expense of their enjoyment of stories which have shaped the development of their cultures.

Case Study 2:
Talking about stories in many languages and cultures

There is a vast repertoire of stories which can be made available in the classroom, whether from collections in print, from visiting storytellers or from the community around the school. This repertoire should include stories which come from a variety of cultures and which were originally – and often still are – in languages other than English. These stories provide a rich resource for education about human societies, offering insights into life in many different communities, and into the complex cultural mix of modern society.

They are also valuable in countering racial or geographical stereotyping, since they reveal much about the nature and complexity of the societies in which they originated. Where pupils are able to tell stories from within their own cultural communities, pupils from minority groups may enhance their own status, and develop a positive self-image.

In a primary school in Luton containing a very high proportion of bilingual children, a storytelling session was structured around the use of home language groups. To begin with, the teacher told an extended personal anecdote in English. This was followed by a childhood story from one of the school's general assistants, told in Urdu. Those children who spoke Urdu then retold this story for the others. Pairs of children speaking the same home language then formed to swap their childhood memories of times that they had got into trouble. These pairs then met up with a pair who spoke a different home language and retold their stories in English. From the children's point of view, the activity gave value to their language and culture, as well as providing a strong stimulus for oral work in English. The teacher was encouraged to see a number of children who had rarely participated in English suddenly revealing confidence in their home language, which began to carry over to English as well. (This example is more fully illustrated in the video cassette which is offered as a companion to this booklet.)

Another storyteller, Inno Sorsy, promotes the use of other tongues, and enhances their status in the stories which she tells. In one storytelling session, she used the fact that there were children of both Greek and Turkish background in the class, and told a story about a Greek man and a Turkish man who travelled widely together. Wherever they went, they used sign language to communicate with local peoples. But when one day their financial resources were low, and both wanted some refreshments in a shop, an argument broke out between them. The Turkish traveller wanted 'uzum' and the Greek traveller wanted 'stafil'. Here is how Inno finished the story:

> . . . all the people in the village came out to see what all the fuss was about. They saw these two grown people hitting and fighting on the ground and rolling in the dust on this hot day.
>
> The villagers didn't know how to speak Greek or Turkish, but they knew that there was a woman, who lived in the village, who was quite wise because she studied languages. So they got her, and they said, 'Please come, because these two travellers . . . they're almost killing each other, and we don't know what for, maybe you can help them.'
>
> So, she came and took the Turkish traveller aside and said, 'My friend, what is this?'
>
> 'Well, I have just been trying to tell this Greek person I am travelling with that what we need is 'uzum'. That's all I need, don't you agree?'
>
> And she said, 'Yes, I do agree. It's the best and wisest thing to do.'
>
> And she took the Greek traveller aside and said, 'What's the problem?'
>
> The Greek travellers said, 'I'm just trying to get it into his head that what we need is "stafil". Don't you agree?'
>
> She said, 'Yes, I agree.'
>
> She got the two of them together, and she said, 'Now look, if you give me your 10p, I will get something which you are both going to like – which is exactly what you both want.'
>
> And they said, 'How can that be? How can 10p buy 'stafil' and 'uzum' at the same time?'
>
> So she said, 'Well, you just wait a minute,' and she went into the shop, and what do you think she came out with?

She came out with a huge bunch of grapes – and, when he saw it, the Turkish traveller said, 'Ah ha. I told you I was right – this wise woman, she understands. What a sensible and reasonable person.'

The Greek traveller said, 'That's what I've been saying all along. This woman understands me. She knows that I'm a sensible and reasonable person.' And so, that's the way, that because they had somebody that understood both languages, they could get together, and they knew they had both been thinking of the same thing all along.

The children then developed their own stories based on similar linguistic misunderstandings.

Case Study 3:
Sharing stories, sharing languages

A class of Year 8 pupils had been working with a visiting storyteller. Her stories had caught their imagination, particularly regarding local and family ghost stories and legends. The class held a storytelling 'lunch', to which members of the local community were invited – the 'entrance fee' was a story. The pupils and their guests shared and traded stories about ghosts; these led to other stories about ghosts, and these in turn led to other stories being told about the locality and from personal and family recollections.

After the 'lunch event', two bilingual pupils worked together on two stories, one of which had been told within the family, the other of which combined a local legend with a community story about an old woman who was a medium. The two pupils were not fully confident either in the writing of English or of Urdu script. Because the stories had originally been told in Urdu, but had been developed in English, they worked together to help one another produce the stories in both scripts. These are the stories:

The possessed woman

There is a lady who lives in my street and she is possessed by a spirit. She is an old lady and she lives with her son and family. She has greenish eyes and is very fair skinned.

One day my mum went to her house and was going to meet this lady whom is possessed by a spirit. Her name is Ma Begum Ji, my mum opened the door and saw that Ma Begum Ji was sitting on the sofa. My mum went by her and said 'Hello' and shook her hand; she replied, 'Hello, how are you?' her voice had changed! It went like a mans. My mum got scared, there were about three four children in the room they got really scared and ran out the room.

Then Ma Begum Ji's daughter-in-law came in and made her lie down. Ma Begum Ji was keep on saying to everyone 'pray pray'!!!

My mum was telling me that when Ma Begum Ji was in Pakistan she was married to a old man. In them days Ma Begum Ji's Ghost used to give her things like money, and gold.

One day her Ghost was giving her some money and her husband saw this happen so he went and told everyone in the village and from that day the ghost has not gave her anything. Now her husband is dead and she has gone back to Pakistan about last month and will be back in about a year's time.
THE END

Shazia Ajmal 5.7.91

Ghost

One day in Pakistan there was a boy, he had a ghost in him. He was acting very strange and he ran away from home. His parents went out looking for him. When they found him they took him to the mosque, and the man at the mosque said, 'He has a ghost inside him, and the man who has done it on him, has a necklace round his neck.'

The man at the mosque told him about a man who could do black magic and they went to him and made him tell them who told you to do black magic on him.

He told him and they went to the man's house and got the necklace off him and burned it. The man then gave the boy a nuther necklace to wear so the ghost will go away.

Majid Hussain 4.7.91

The written texts were displayed in the classroom, and the pupils read and told the stories to their friends. The class and their teacher recognised that the stories had brought together the strands of storytelling which they had been working on: family, community and ghost stories. The bilingual work had elicited and encouraged higher achievements in both Speaking and Listening, and in Writing, than the two pupils had previously demonstrated.

Case Study 4:
Stories for all

It is important for children with two or more languages to express themselves in whichever language they wish, and to understand that their language and culture are valued. Storytelling offers an ideal opportunity for this. Storytelling can be equally liberating for children with different physical, aural or visual disabilities or sensory loss. Here, for example, is an account of one boy's work.

Matthew suffers from cerebral palsy. Although he finds speaking a real effort, he is a very bright, determined child, and takes part in as many activities with his peers as possible. On this occasion, his teacher told the class her version of the story, 'Ma Liang and the

Magic Brush' (see extracts of transcript, opposite). Matthew joined in the storytelling with interest and enthusiasm, listening keenly to the story and then trying to retell it, including a dramatised retelling to a group of younger children in the school. Matthew then went to a word-processor, where he produced his version of the story, which we have printed after the opening section of the teacher's original telling (see opposite).

Notice how the original story has stimulated Matthew to retain in his writing some of the conversational feel of the told story ('she only drawd with stics stwns eeven') and its condensed and compact form, even while retelling it in a word-processed form. It seems in some ways as if Matthew has needed the help of the word-processor in order fully to communicate his 'speech'.

In this instance, a story told by the teacher was the initial stimulus. The directness of the situation, with the Ma Liang story being communicated without the interference of any text, seems here to have helped Matthew (and the other pupils who were participating) to achieve a similar direct quality in his writing. Other factors were at work too. Once the teacher had completed the telling, she asked the group to 'reconstruct' the story together, piece by piece. Their enthusiasm to do so was clearly visible, including Matthew whose great efforts to contribute were listened to by all the rest. Then the teacher suggested that the group might like to retell, or enact with a narrator, the story for a younger class. Once again, the quality of discussion and the level of contribution were evidence of the way that the narrative, with its magical ingredients, had caught the pupils' imaginations. The story was duly reworked and presented that afternoon. Interestingly, one of the most reticent and unconfident pupils was prepared to take on the narrator role. Storytelling had provided this group of pupils with a clear structure to work within, but also a genuine challenge that they were prepared to take up. It opened doors and revealed potential that could be seized and built upon.

In *Curriculum Guidance 3 – The Whole Curriculum* – the National Curriculum Council states that:

'In order to make access to the whole curriculum a reality for all pupils, schools need to foster a climate in which equality of opportunity is supported by a policy to which the whole school subscribes and in which positive attitudes to gender equality, cultural diversity and special needs of all kinds are actively promoted.'

Teacher's original telling of 'Ma Liang and the Magic Brush'

Once upon a time, a long time ago, in a country called China, there lived a little boy called Ma Liang. And he loved to draw. But he was so poor he couldn't afford a brush. So, when he drew, he often used stones, or sticks, or even his fingers and while he was drawing he used to think to himself, 'Oh, I wish I could afford a brush. I could draw much better with a brush.' And suddenly, one day, while he was drawing on the ground with his fingers, an old man with a long, white beard appeared. And he said to Ma Liang, 'Don't be frightened, Ma Liang. For I have brought you a magic brush. But you must only draw pictures for poor people.' And with that he disappeared. So Ma Liang picked up the magic brush and he started to draw.

Matthew's written version

(Matthew's reason for changing Ma Liang from a male to a female character in his telling was because when the class improvised the story a girl took on the part of Ma Liang.)

Marleang & shee magik brush.
once upon a time ther was a littl girl cold Marleang and shee loveed to dowe and shee had no brush and shee onle drawd with stics stwns eeven her fingers but shee wisht shee had a brush one day wiylst marleang was drawing a man caym and sed maliang downt be fritoned I will giv you a majic brush but onele draw for por pepl
and he drawd a cocrl and it floo off. then shee saw a layde choppinng trees dawn but the ax was to blunt so shee
drawd her an ax and it bicaym a rell ax.
then he saw an man puling a plaw so shee draw a bufalo

and he sed thenkyou marlian now it's alot esa. now the king hered abut marlian and sent for her and the king sed draw mee a tree with gold couns on it and marlian sed "NO"! I onli draw for por pipl you yormanchensty are rich.

and the king sed thow her in the deepist dunjon and maliang thot haw to get out and shee draw a cee and it fitted the looc and shee escayped and the gards sor her and thay thot I must be seeing things but stil thay chayst arfter her maliang draw a hors and a howl and the gards fell in and thay wer never seen agen and marlang toled the vilejers her story

Matthew

Rebuilding stories

From a given story:

- Invent an earlier episode

- Create a fresh ending

- Change first person/personal to third person/artefact

- Drop a character/add a character

- Change a character's behaviour

- Make a hero a heroine/a heroine a hero

- Change features or sympathies within a story, e.g. foolish behaviour becomes courageous

- Story characters tell their versions: i) hot seating; ii) freeze framing; iii) role play; iv) interviews.

- Genre – changing fairy tale, e.g. murder mystery

- Change a geography/historical setting

In this chapter we have tried to show how storytelling can help to promote these positive attitudes by:

- helping pupils to recognise and, if necessary, change stereotypical aspects of narratives, in so doing building up their awareness of a fuller range of roles and possibilities for characters as a contribution to the establishment of their own self-image;

- encouraging the use of stories from a wide variety of cultures;

- encouraging pupils to tell and retell stories in their own languages;

- encouraging pupils to contribute stories which draw positively on their own cultural and community experiences;

- providing access to language development and to the meanings of stories for pupils with special educational needs.

In the first five chapters of this book we have put the case for storytelling as a powerful way of developing language and learning. Through the case studies we have illustrated something of the range of possible narrative styles that might be built into the curriculum. We have seen how valuable a resource stories can be for helping pupils to give shape to their experiences, and for deepening their understanding of the world. We have shown how both pupils and teachers can grow in confidence as tellers of stories themselves. Chapter 6 is designed to help you to take the next step and to plan for approaches to storytelling yourself.

In many ways these chapters document the way that storytelling began to emerge as an aspect of oracy that caught the imagination of pupils and teachers alike in the National Oracy Project. We have gathered evidence over the last few years of a growing number of teachers who have taken that first step, put the book aside and told stories. Local storytelling groups have been formed; professional storytellers are working in increasing numbers in schools and colleges. As one primary teacher said of storytelling: 'It's a common bond, between me and my children – the stories we share together.'

We hope that some of this has rubbed off and that your imagination has been caught too.

SIX

Practical resources for using and developing stories

Introduction

This chapter contains a collection of materials and further resources which will give practical guidance to those interested in introducing storytelling into their classroom or in developing their understanding and use of it. This material comes in the form of:

● a series of five discrete checklists which deal with how and where to find stories, how to become a storyteller, an outline of the audiences available for storytelling, how to arrange a storytelling event and a list of ways into storytelling.

● an extensive list of resources, which gathers together academic books on storytelling, guidebooks on storytelling written by practising storytellers, collections of stories and audio material available to supplement the voices present in the classroom.

In addition to the checklists mentioned above, five display sheets and illustrations which feature in the other chapters of this book can be used in a similar way: they are to be found on pp. 18-9, 22-3, 40-1, 52-3 and 66-7. Here are some suggestions for their use:

– They can serve as the basis of a display on aspects of storytelling and narrative. The checklists can be supplemented with photographs and captions, pupils' stories, comments and reflections, teacher commentary . . . and the whole can be presented to a range of different audiences.

– They can be given to pupils and used to stimulate classroom investigation. For example, the first checklist presented here would allow pupils to research the stories that surround them and the sources of stories in their community.

— They can be used as a device for carrying out a review or audit of the storytelling activity in individual classrooms, departments or schools. You could, for example, compare the suggestions given in 'Involving the community' on pp. 22-3 with your own practice over a fixed period of time.

— They can be used as material for an in-service session. A follow-up meeting would allow teachers to share and review the evidence from their classrooms.

— They can be used to help you plan your storytelling activities. Such activities could range from using the ideas on checklist 10 to get you started, to planning a large scale storytelling event using checklist 8.

— They can be copied and put into a ring file, the sheets forming the basis of a growing and shared bank of storytelling materials which can be edited and supplemented over time.

Checklist 1. Stories are everywhere

Stories in many languages

Children can be asked to form 'home language' groups for the first stage of work which involves telling and retelling anecdotes. Each group chooses one of the stories and then retells it, in English, in new 'mixed' language groups. Bilingual tapes of stories can be made (with stories in translation) and a collection of traditional tales from many cultures and in different languages can also be produced.

Memories

> I can remember coming to live at Bradford ... it stands out in my mind, this. We always wore clogs, you see, in the country, and when we came to live in Bradford on the farm, the farmer's daughter was to take me to school, and her and her friend saw me coming and because I had clogs on they wouldn't walk with me ... and I've never forgotten it.

Stories from many cultures

The sharing of stories from many cultures can contribute to a richer, harmonious society. Compare and contrast the similarities and differences that exist in stories such as Snow White with Sitand Lakham (Bengali) or Raj Rasalu (Punjabi) with St George & the Dragon.

Dilemma tales

Traditionally used in order to draw out debate in the community or village, dilemma tales dealt with different problems – moral, ethical, legal or social, and gave the elders the chance to show their knowledge; they also helped parents deal with unruly offspring. Dilemma tales leave the listener with a problem to be solved through debate with others.

Jokes

These are stories too. Take the tale of the Wide-Mouthed Frog ... going through the jungle ... happy, contented, ebullient ... meets other animals ... chats about the weather, happiness, food, etc. with them ... then encounters a grumpy lion looking for food ... trying to help, the frog asks what his favourite food is ... 'Wide-Mouthed Frogs,' comes the reply. 'You don't see many of those around here,' replies the frog with pursed lips!

Rumours and apocryphal stories

Overheard any day, anywhere. Some of doubtful authority (hence apocryphal):

'... there it was, as large as life'

'... and do you know where they found him ... ?'

'... so she threw it at him.'

Myths, folktales, fables and legends

Distinctions have now become blurred between myths, folktales, fables and legends. Traditionally, myths are stories of gods or heroes: Zeus, Ra, Perseus, Jason. In fables, animals and inanimate objects often act and speak as humans. Aesop is the most obvious example here, but many other sources exist. The ingredients of folktales are familiar to us all – very good/bad characters, repetitive language, simple plots, fantastic events. Legends originally contained the truths and untruths surrounding a person such as a saint or a wise man.

Anecdotes

Listen to the children in your class tell you about things that have happened to them:

'You'll never guess what happened to me when ...'

'Do you know what my dad did at the weekend ...?'

'... the other day, right, a neighbour of ours ...'

Encourage the listeners to question the storyteller in order to find out more:

'What happened next?'

'How did he manage to get out?'

'How did you feel?'

Accumulators

Many stories and poems for young children start in a simple way and grow or accumulate characters as the story progresses. The Giant Turnip, The Enormous Watermelon, The Gingerbread Boy, The Very Hungry Caterpillar are all examples of this.

Narrative accounts of work

Children are often asked to explain to a group or class how they made a model or how a problem was solved. These are stories too.

'Well, first of all we had to find out …'.

'Sam and I decided to work together, and he had this idea which was to stick …'.

'I painted the background first – well, I printed it really with a sponge – and when that had dried I sketched in …'

Number stories

Numbers have magical and powerful associations in many stories. Take the number 3, for example: three wishes, three witches, three tasks, the third son or daughter. 7 and 13 also feature frequently in stories.

Personal/Family Histories

'… my father had six other brothers. Two stayed in Ireland, and four went to America. Now things start to get interesting, because one of the three who went to America got married and had two children before he died. Then his brother married his widow.'

Where will you find some stories?

Checklist 2. Becoming a storyteller

Teachers

- Choose a story you like, can relate to and feel comfortable with: a folktale, local legend, personal anecdote, a story you've usually heard or read aloud. A simple theory is best, or one you've simplified for the particular purpose of oral retelling.

- Tell the story to yourself, the mirror, your family, the dog while out walking, anyone who'll listen. No need to memorise every word: you want to make the story your own – in your words, for your audiences. Try telling the story in different ways, formally and informally.

  Practice and experience enable the storyteller to bring out the full potential of a story.[1]

- Do have the opening sequences very clearly prepared in your head, so you can begin confidently. It may be helpful to visualise the story: see it as a sequence of vivid moving pictures.

- Try to tell any story publicly within a very few days of learning and preparing it, to avoid staleness.

- Remember, while telling a story, you've no book and, while that has risks, it also frees you to turn that story into a directly personal experience for each of your listeners. You can adapt your telling to suit your audience as part of your preparation, and spontaneously as part of the actual presentation.

- Pair up with a sympathetic colleague to swap stories and practise telling to each other.

- Tell a class a story in pre-determined sections, pausing after each, asking children in pairs to consider what will happen next. This gives you a breathing space and a chance to check the next part before asking for their suggestions and moving on.

- Reflect on how you've told a story:

  - physical gestures (important but distracting if overdone);

  - stand or sit (what differences does this make?);

---

[1] Colwell, E. (1991) *Story-Telling* (The Thimble Press)

- eye contact (with the whole of your audience);
- voice changes (for different characters; for changes of pace, volume, pitch, intensity, accent);
- breathing (is it under control?);
- could you tape record your tellings for personal evaluation afterwards?

Keep a growing collection of the outlines of your stories in a note book or on cards for revision purposes. It is useful also to record the source, in case you need to check details.

Involve a whole school staff or department in preparing one story each to tell to their own and each other's classes. This ensures children hear a good range of stories and each teacher can develop a skill at telling that story and experiment with varying it for different audiences.

Put the book you've learned your story from well away from you when you're telling it – that way, you'll not be tempted back into reading.

Advice to children
Chain stories
After hearing a story, children retell it, each contributing a bit, then passing on to the next person. There could be a symbolic story stick or conch passed on; whoever holds this holds the telling-ground.

Words and pictures
After hearing a story each pupil folds a piece of paper in eight 'boxes'. In each the pupil draws a relevant cartoon, plus a caption to cover the whole story. This new 'text' is used to support a retelling of the story.

Bone-patterns
Pupils condense a story to seven key words, each a trigger to retelling a section of a story.

Babble/gabble
In pairs, children tell each other a story they have heard or tried to learn as quickly as possible in a fixed time, maybe 90 seconds.

Story-pairs
Response-partners can offer considerable mutual support when rehearsing or telling stories publicly, say, to a previously unknown

audience. Partnerships can be developed through such activities as 'Show & Tell', where one partner tells the story and the other provides gestures, which the teller immediately copies. Roles can swap half way through.

Finish it!
The teacher stops the telling of a story before the end and invites children in pairs to improvise an ending. These can then be shared between pairs and/or the whole class.

A's & B's
The teacher divides the class into two halves, A and B, then tells each half of the class a different story. Pupils practise retelling this story (see 'babble/gabble' above) to partners in their own half before pairs from A and B are formed to exchange their stories.

Story-swapping
In pairs, children exchange personal anecdotes on some given theme; pairs find fresh partners and tell the story they've just heard as if it happened to them. Repeat the process for as long as it sustains fun and interest.

2, 4, 8
Again in pairs, children swap personal stories. Pairs then make fours, exchanging one story from each pair. Fours make eights for the same process. Eights can become half class groups, then finally, as a whole class, volunteers tell their stories.

Oral drafting
Set up an audio or video tape recorder in a separate area for practice and critical playback. Tapes and rehearsals and more public tellings could be used regularly for assessment, pupil reflection and self-assessment.

Conferencing
The teacher sets time aside to work with groups of children to hear them rehearsing their storytelling, offering advice and support as necessary.

The story store
To encourage participation by younger children, a teacher needs to build up a collection of puppets, masks and cut out figures to use to support their telling.

New tales for old
Invite older pupils to rework a story from some fresh perspective, e.g:

– set it in a fresh historical period;

– set it in the children's home town ... yesterday;

– individual pupils assume the persona of one of the tale's characters and retell it;

– retell it to encourage sympathy for different characters;

– change the gender of the central figure(s).

Becoming experts
Involve children in preparing tellings for a specific audience and purpose, e.g. as storytellers-in-residence to younger pupils as part of a school's Book Week. (An excellent account of such a process is available on the video 'Children as Storytellers' by Tony Aylwin at Thames Polytechnic, 1989.)

Checklist 3. Audiences and environments

Two children swap stories.

Each child retells a story to the next child in a chain of storytelling.

One child tells or retells a story to a small group of friends.

Children of different ages share stories with one another.

The teacher tells a story to a small group of children, who retell it to others.

Two children swap stories then retell their partner's stories to other children.

Audiences for storytelling

Explore a range and variety of audiences in the storytelling, so that teachers, children and other participants can play varying roles.

Invite parents into the school to tell stories and to listen to the children's stories.

One child plays his tape-recorded story to others.

Each teacher in the school learns one story, and then tells it to several classes in turn.

Environments

Think in advance about which children will be involved in the telling, and where and how they will work. What will the other children be doing?

Get all the participants seated, at the same level for good eye contact, in a relatively self-enclosed space.

Groups of chairs, gymnastic mats, book corners, role play areas, sets of cushions, easy chairs, are all good resources for designating particular places for storytelling.

Find space which groups can use for a short time – the library, a drama area, the school hall – and lay out the furniture to match the size of groups.

The story environment

It is important to plan the organisation and layout of the classroom, hall or space being used for storytelling. The atmosphere should be comfortable and unthreatening.

Help the groups by providing props, some costume or a setting, and making sure that those telling the stories are directing their voices to their audience.

Think about how long the storytelling will last, and how all the participants can share in the process of making and telling the story.

Set the mood and atmosphere with music, lighting or an introduction that helps the children to create an imaginative world.

Checklist 4. A storytelling event

A storytelling event

A good way to gain most from storytelling is to work with colleagues and to commit a significant period of time to work which is involved with storytelling. In a primary school, this can be done by several teachers, or the whole staff, committing themselves to storytelling for a period such as a week, in which many stories can be explored in depth while they enrich pupils' learning in other areas of the curriculum. In a secondary school, timetabling and staffing commitments may rule out so lengthy a period of time. However, with the support of colleagues it may be possible to extend work beyond the ordinary limits of lesson times – to two days' special timetabling, for example. Attention to storytelling could be paid during other events such as a School Book Week.

Planning a storytelling event

There is no one way to set about doing this. How you approach it depends on many variables, e.g. whether there is a tradition of storytelling in the school and whether liaison with other schools and the local community is already established. In your planning, consideration should be given to:

— the classes/pupils to be involved;

— what involvement the children will have in the planning;

— what use will be made of visiting storytellers, e.g. parents, the local community, a professional storyteller, other pupils, etc;

— other potential audiences, e.g. other schools, classes, parents, community groups, etc;

— what kinds of stories will be told, e.g. thematic, from particular countries, 'dilemma' stories;

— what school resources (staffing rooms, other working areas, equipment, finance) will be available;

— how and where the stories will be told and retold;

— what areas of the curriculum are to be covered or enriched during the event;

— how the work will be reflected on and evaluated by the staff and pupils;

– how the outcomes will be recorded;

– how the work will be followed up.

Your views on these issues will help to inform the 'shape' of the event, e.g. when certain key events will occur, and when time should be available for the pupils to be working by themselves. You should be able to marshal the various resources, audiences, etc within this general shape. Most schools which have conducted such events have found it valuable to begin and end with activities which give status and impetus to the remainder of the work.

It may be useful to use the planning schedule below as a guide:

General Planning

Schools/classes involved:

Staff involved:

Name, address and contact telephone number of storyteller, if used:

Curriculum areas/work to be covered:

Tasks to be completed before the event:

Schedule of events

Dates of storytelling events:

Session One:

Session Two:

Session Three:

Session Four:

Follow-up:

Evaluation/Reflection:

Checklist 5. Starters – a menu of possibilities

Story-starters

Chain-whispers

One player whispers a possible story opening to another, who whispers what he or she has heard to another, and so on, until the whole group has received and passed on the line. See what it has now become and begin a shared story with the new opening.

One word only

Begin 'Once ... upon ... a ... time ...', with each player saying just one word to build up a whole story.

Fortunately ... unfortunately

One player begins with, 'There was once a ... who ...'. The next player (or their partner) adds an episode beginning, 'Unfortunately ...'. The next player must begin, 'Fortunately ...' and so on to build up the story-line. Don't allow repetitions or sudden deaths!

Chain-story

Begin 'In the city of Rome there was a street'. The next player might say, 'In the city of Rome there was a street, and in that street there was a fountain.' And so on, with each player adding a fresh detail to build up a large 'still picture'. Ordinary details are better than the fantastical.

Guided fantasies

To relax a class and change the atmosphere, ask them to sit comfortably, preferably with their eyes closed, then give them an outline description (five minutes at the most) of a story-setting. Leave the filling-out of the detail to their imaginations and allow pauses for this imaginative work. You might even include questions in your outline to which you will seek answers in any subsequent discussion.

Make a circle

Pass the buck

Only the person holding the 'buck' may speak. The first holder begins a story, then passes the buck to the next player, or throws it randomly across the circle. Whoever catches it must continue the story.

Buzz

The first player says '1', the next '2', the next '3' and so on. As soon as '5' or any multiple of 5 is reached 'buzz' replaces the number: so 25 is buzz. Add 'fizz' for 3 or its multiples to play 'Fizz Buzz', so that, for example, 15 is 'fizz buzz'.

I want to tell a story about …

Each player repeats this opening, then contributes some fresh idea. Collect these for display. Re-organised, they make good poems/ posters, and children can choose any of the given items to develop a story.

A was a Queen called Anne

The first player says this, the next says, for example, 'B bullied/ boasted to/baked bread for her'; the next might say, 'C cuddled/ chatted to/crocheted a coat for her', and so on through the alphabet.

The headteacher's cat

Another alphabet game, with the first player saying, 'The head-teacher's cat is an a— cat and its name is A—', the next offering adjectives and names for B and so on, once again, through the alphabet.

Rounds

Begin, for example, with, 'My favourite piece of clothing is ...', or 'If I could go anywhere ...', or 'The thing about telling a story I like best/ find most difficult is ...'. This is a good ice-breaker, which encourages everyone to contribute.

Brain teasers and memory games

Lists

Begin, for example, with 'There once was a king who hated —'. Each player adds an item to the growing list, but first must repeat in correct order the items previous players have contributed.

Telling lies

Working in small groups, each pupil must offer one fresh untruth about a given object/place/person, e.g. 'The Eiffel Tower is made of chocolate/... has gone to Madrid/... was planted by Venusians', etc.

Tall stories

Pairs of children are asked to brainstorm ideas for a story based on a 'What if ...?' proposition, e.g. '... grass grew tall as children?', '... the sea could talk?', '... the world lost all its clocks?'

In my story ...

One player thinks of a category or concept and offers examples of this by saying, 'In my story there is — but no —'. For example, '...there are floods but no ice', '...there is coffee but no cups'. The rest must guess what the category or concept is (in this case the story has only words including a double letter, though, given the examples so far, it might also have been the concept of wetness).

Smiles and frowns

Two players leave the room, having been told that while they are out those remaining will make up a story which they must find out about on their return by asking questions. Once the pair is gone, explain to the others that there will be no story, that when they return the pair will 'make up' the story by being told 'yes' when they ask a question with a smile, and 'no' when they frown or look serious when asking it. Let the fun begin!

What are you doing?

One player mimes any action, e.g. playing a trombone; the next asks 'What are you doing?'; the first must give any incorrect answer, e.g. 'I'm walking my dog'; at which point the other must mime this, and so on through the whole group.

Rhythms, rhymes and chants

Stones

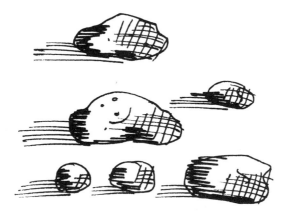

Each player has a stone; these are passed round the circle to establish a rhythm. Add an accompanying chant, e.g. players' names, words linked by association, items in different languages; experiment with changes of speed and direction. One stone-passing game is 'La-di-DA;. the chant is 'La-di-DA/La-di-DA/La-di-da-di-da-di-DA'. The stones are held in the right hand and passed clockwise on the main 'DA' beat; the trick in the third line is to move your stone to the beat but not drop it until the main 'DA' comes.

Rhyme time

Begin a collection for shared chanting (and accompanying clapping); these can be from books or from children's own street and playground names. Here's one from the Caribbean:

'Where's your mama gone?'
'She's gone down town.'
'Did she take any money?'
'Yes, she took ten pound.'
'When your mama come back, what she going to bring back?'
'Hats and socks and shoes and frocks.'

Overtures

The storyteller Hugh Lupton suggests that before a story is told something should occur to separate the everyday world from the storytelling event – a whistle, a tambourine, even a whisper.

Tick-tock

Played in a circle. One player (A) begins, 'This is a tick', looking to person on their left (B); B replies 'A what?'. A replies, 'A tick'. B says to C on their left, 'This is a tick.' C replies, 'A what?'. B goes back to A saying, 'A what?' A repeats, 'A tick'. This is then passed down to C, and so on clockwise around the circle, with the response-chain growing all the time. Meanwhile … once the 'Tick' has reached C or D, A turns to the person on the right and says, 'This is a Tock'. The original pattern is now built up in an anti-clockwise direction. Watch out for the moment when 'Tick' and 'Tock' meet – and hopefully pass safely on!

All of us are storytellers

With young pupils a chant such as this can be used (and adapted) to create a positive atmosphere for storytelling. Lines can be added which bring focus and attention to the next phase of the work, or to the next storyteller.

Selective bibliography: books for storytelling

These books contain versions of stories which have been taken directly from, or with great regard for, the oral tradition.

ABRAHAMS, R. *African Folktales* Pantheon
APPIAH, P. *The Pineapple Child* (Ashanti) André Deutsch
BRIGGS, K. *The Vanishing People* (British Folk & Fairy) Pantheon
BUSHNAQ, I. *Arab Folktales* (Penguin Folklore Library) Penguin
CANDAPPA, B. *Tales of South Asia* Ginn & Co
DANNAHER, K. *Folktales of the Irish Countryside* Mercier
GARNER, A. *British Fairy Tales* Collins
GLASSIE, H. *Irish Folktales* (Penguin Folklore Library) Penguin
HALLWORTH, G. *Mouth Open, Story Jump Out* (Trinidad & Tobago) Methuen Press
JACOBS, J. *English Fairy Tales* Penguin
LENIHAN, E. *Stories of Old Ireland For Children* Mercier
MANNING–SANDERS, R. *Folk and Fairy Tales* Methuen
MERCER, J. *Stories of Vanishing Peoples* Alison & Busby
PEPPER, D. *A Book of Tall Tales* Oxford University Press
RIORDAN, J. *Russian Gypsy Tales* Canongate
SHAH, I. *World Tales* Harcourt Brace Jovanovich
WILLIAMSON, D. *Fireside Tales of Travellers' Children* Canongate
WILLIAMSON, D. and L. *A Thorn in the King's Foot* (Penguin Folklore Library) Penguin
WILLIAMSON, D. and L. *Elijah's Violin and Other Jewish Tales* (Penguin Folklore Library) Penguin

Audio cassette tape collections of traditional stories

(Details correct at the time of going to press)

(P) indicates suitable for primary age range
(S) indicates suitable for secondary age range

CAMPBELL, J. *On the hip of Sliabh Gullion* (S)
Spring Records, 50 Shore Road, Rostrevor, Co Down, Ireland
COMPANY OF STORYTELLERS *Winter Tales* (and the tapes of Lupton,
   Heggarty and Clayton) (S)
3 Church Terrace, Alysham, Norfolk, NR11 6EU
Two Tongue Tales (P & S)
Helen East, 29 Gleneldon Road, Streatham, London, SW16 2AX
EAST/WILSON *A Word in Your Ear* (P)
Helen East (address as above)
HALLWORTH, G. *A Ball of Fire* (P)
Culture Waves, PO Box 1301, London, N16 5YS
LENIHAN, E. *Storyteller 2* (S)
Eddie Lenihan, Crusheen, Co Clare, Ireland
ROBERTSON, S. *Nippit Fit Clipplit Fit* (P)
Stanley Robertson, 161 Marchburn Drive, Aberdeen, Scotland
ROSEN/GRIFFITHS *That'd be Telling* (P & S) Cambridge University
   Press
WILLIAMSON, D. *Mary and the Seal People* (P)
Linda Williamson, Falfield Bank, Peat Inn, Cupar, Fife, KY15 5LL
WILLIAMSON, R. *The Fisherman's Son and the Gruagach of Tricks* (P)
BCM 4797, London, WC1N 3XX

'The Lute Player' is included in *Changing Stories* published by the
English and Media Centre, 1984.

Thanks to Helen East for this list of sources.

Thanks to Rick Wilson for supplying the audio cassette details.

Further bibliography

AYLWIN, T. *Storytelling and Education*
AYLWIN, T. and PETERS, J. *Children as Storytellers* (30 minute video cassette) Available from The School of Primary Education, Thames Polytechnic, Avery Hill Campus, London SE9 2PQ

The booklet suggests ways of working with storytelling in school and also includes helpful factual information on currently influential storytellers. The video film shows the processes a class of upper junior children go through as they prepare to be storytellers to infant children at the school's Book Week.

BARTON, B. (1986) *Tell Me Another: Storytelling and Reading Aloud at Home, at School and in the Community* Heinemann (Canada)

An essential guide to the teacher wanting to begin or to develop storytelling. Written by a Canadian storyteller, the book offers clear, sensible advice on selecting stories for telling, how to learn and prepare stories and how to introduce a range of related activities. Much of the advice is anchored to stories included in the text which in themselves provide excellent pieces to tell.

THE CENTRE FOR LEARNING IN PRIMARY EDUCATION (1983) *Stories in the Multicultural Primary Classroom: Supporting Children's Learning of English as a Second Language* Harcourt, Brace, Jovanovich Ltd

Although explicitly targeted on second language learners, this extremely practical booklet has a lot to say about story for all children. A mass of story-related activities are included, and a number of story-texts for teachers and children to use. Also an excellent sequence of reviews of picture and story books suitable for telling. (Also available from the Centre for Learning in Primary Education, Webber Row Teachers' Centre, London, SE1 8QW.)

COLWELL, E. (1991) *Storytelling* The Thimble Press, Station Road, South Woodchester, Stroud, Gloucestershire, GL5 5EQ

As further proof of the revival of interest in storytelling Eileen Colwell's classic is now back in print over 10 years after its first publication. Aimed at teachers and tellers working with five to pre-teen age range, it is a rich and at once very useful book, full of sensible, helpful advice and practical suggestions. Above all, Eileen Colwell writes in a way that persuades her readers that telling stories is a skill they could all accomplish successfully.

COTTERILL, L. and EAST, H. (eds.) (1990) *Directory of Storytellers* Available from Helen East, 29 Gleneldon Road, Streatham, London SW16 7AX

An indispensable booklet listing storytellers available to work throughout the country, with a brief but helpful account of particular skills, cultural emphases and working preferences of each teller. Also included are several excellent background articles.

THE ENGLISH AND MEDIA CENTRE (1984) *Making Stories* and *Changing Stories* The English and Media Centre (available from NATE, Birley School Annexe, Fox Lane Site, Frecheville, Sheffield, S12 4WY)

Two rich and deservedly influential books on the subject. Both offer a wide range of stories, including stories with clear thematic links from around the world and also different versions of the same story. Stories are accompanied by suggested activities and the whole forms an excellent basis for any school or department seeking to develop a curriculum for narrative.

MEDLICOTT, M. (ed.) (1989) *By Word of Mouth: The Revival of Storytelling* Available from C4 Broadside Productions, 17b Finsbury Park Road, London N4 2LA.

A package of the four-part Channel Four series on storytelling, on video cassette with accompanying booklet and background notes. The material covers anecdotes and articulating experience, developing storytelling skills and the passing on of stories through the oral tradition.

MORGAN, J. and RINVOLUCRI, M. (1983) *Once Upon a Time: Using Stories in the Language Classroom* Cambridge University Press

Intended as a handbook for teachers of English as a second language, this is also an excellent collection of ideas for classroom activities related to story-making and developing children's powers of narration. Very well organised, the book also includes over 70 'story skeletons' for telling and retelling.

ROSEN, B. (1988) *And None of it Was Nonsense: The Power of Storytelling in School* Mary Glasgow Publications

A book of real vision rooted in the demanding classroom realities of a North London Secondary school. Betty Rosen describes introducing storytelling – traditional and tales from mythology – into the English curriculum and includes several examples of the pupils' responses to her invitation to retell these stories.

ROSEN, B. (1992) *Shapers and Polishers – Teachers as Storytellers* Mary Glasgow Publications

Having looked at children's narrative powers in her first book, here the author considers the narrative skill of teachers, arguing, and offering compelling evidence that they are 'a very talented lot.' A heartening and very readable book, it includes in Part 3 a dozen complete stories for classroom use.

ROSEN, H. (1985) *Stories and Meanings* NATE Publications, NATE, Birley School Annexe, Fox Lane Site, Frecheville, Sheffield S12 4WY

'No-one tells us why language development should not include as a central component getting better at telling and responding to stories of many different kinds.' Exactly, and in this pamphlet the author seeks commitedly and vigorously to accord story its proper place both in school and for all our lives.

STEELE, M. (ed.) (1989) *Traditional Tales* The Thimble Press (for details, see Colwell, E.)

Compiled by Mary Steele, this book contains an excellent range of stories and anthologies for classroom use.

WEIR, L. (ed.) (1989) *Telling the Tale, a Storytelling Guide* YLG Pamphlet No. 29, The Library Association, Youth Library's Group

A collection of six articles, each written by a practising storyteller. Inevitably, given the diverse authorship, a bit of a hotch potch of ideas, approaches and suggestions. There is nevertheless more than enough here to enthuse the intending teacher-teller and sustain that enthusiasm via the variety of strategies and follow-up activities included.

WELLS, G. (1987) *The Meaning Makers: Children Learning Language and Using Language to Learn* Hodder & Stoughton

Not wholly about storytelling, this book nevertheless has some very precise things to say about its essential place in any child's language entitlement. Chapter 8, 'What's in a Story', and Chapter 10, 'The Sense of Story', are the most useful starting points, the latter arguing a powerful case for the need for stories and storytelling 'in all subjects of the curriculum'.